Life After
Deployment

Military families share
reunion stories and advice

Karen M. Pavlicin

author of Surviving Deployment:
A guide for military families

Elva Resa ∗ Saint Paul

Life After Deployment: Military families share reunion stories and advice
© 2007 by Karen M. Pavlicin
All rights reserved.

Cover design by Andermax Studios. Back cover photo by Wendy Woods.
Personal stories used with permission. Some names have been changed.
Comments by Dr. Colson and Dr. Morse courtesy of TriWest Healthcare
Alliance. The intent of this book is to share stories and provide ideas to
military families. Each situation is unique and you should seek professional
or medical advice as appropriate.

Library of Congress Cataloging-in-Publication Data

Pavlicin, Karen.
  Life after deployment : military families share reunion stories and advice
  / Karen M. Pavlicin.
    p. cm.
  ISBN-13: 978-0-9657483-7-7 (pbk.)
  ISBN-10: 0-9657483-7-5 (pbk.)
  1. Military spouses—United States. 2. Military dependents—United States.
    I. Title.
  UB403.P35 2007
  355.1'20973—dc22

2006039764

Printed in United States of America.
    4 5 6 7 8 9 10

Elva Resa Publishing
http://www.elvaresa.com
http://www.lifeafterdeployment.com

To Lana, who killed the chickens,

and to everyone who waits

To my son, Alexander,

who makes every homecoming special

To the service members of the United States Armed Forces:

make us proud,

come home safe,

love us with all your heart,

and let us love you right back

Contents

Author's Note .... *vii*

Introduction: The Answers *1*
    Laugh, Love, and Buy More Underwear 2
    Make Time for You 6
    Help Your Whole Being 12
    Maintain Strong Relationships 20
    Support Children 22
    The Mega Answer List 29

Chapter One: Planning the Rendezvous *35*
    Reflecting on Your Experience 40
    Getting Ready for the Big Day 44
    What to Expect in the First Days 49
    A New Beginning 59

Chapter Two: Learning to Dance Again *61*
    Different Worlds 67
    Intimacy 70
    New Kind of Communication 73
    New Routines 75
    Rebuilding Relationships Through the Changes 77
    When Is It Time to Seek Help? 80
    Happy Reunions 81

Chapter Three: Stress and Other Things We Worry About *83*
    What Service Members Need to Adjust at Home 85
    Getting Help 88

Anger 88
Anxiety 90
Depression 91
Post-Traumatic Stress Disorder 93
Kid Stress 99
Benefits of Talking with a Chaplain 101

Chapter Four: Caregiving and Grief 109
Caregiver Perspective 110
Grief Perspective 112
Common Symptoms of Grief.. 130
Working Through Grief... 132
A Few Things I Have Learned 137

Chapter Five: Continuing the Journey 143
Much of Life is Perspective... 144
Rebuilding with Your Spouse 146
Creating Trust with Children 146
Connecting with Teens 148
Exploring New Relationships Between Parents
and Service Members 149
Coping with News of a Pending Deployment or
Feelings About Going Back 150
The Next Chapter in the Journey 153

Appendix: Resources for Your Happily Ever After.................. 155
Deployment and Reunion 155
Military Family Centers and Support Groups 158
General Military Life 159
Associations and Support Services................................. 162
Service Branches 163
Military Services Relief Societies.................................... 164
Parenting 165
Anger, Depression, Stress, and PTSD 166
Living with Injuries 168
Death and Grief 171
Hotlines and Community Resources 177
Peer Military Groups and Veteran's Organizations 179

Author's Note

When I began to talk with military families about a book on reunions, I quickly realized that the most powerful part of the book idea was the stories themselves. As Lana Schmidtke, one of the Army National Guard wives I interviewed, wrote in an email to me:

> No one can ever prepare you for what the soldiers went through while they were away from home nor can the soldiers ever be prepared for the changes and experiences their families went through. But being able to read others' stories about what it was like for them will give everyone who reads your book the comfort of knowing that they are not alone during deployment and reunion. They'll know there are many others who have walked the same journey and did, in fact, survive. Those stories will help people know that although they may feel they are traveling that journey alone, there are many out there who have also traveled it and are still traveling with them in their hearts.

Each person I interviewed eagerly told his or her story for just that reason: *maybe my experience will help another military family.*

The group interviewed was diverse. Family members from all branches of service gave input, including Army, Air Force, Navy, Marines, Coast Guard, National Guard, Reserves, and Individual Ready Reserve. Interviewees included military service members who were deployed after 9/11; children as young as five years old through college age; spouses from age nineteen to forty-eight; siblings, friends, and fiancées; and parents who had a son or daughter deployed. Service members included single, married, and divorced; enlisted and officer; active duty and reservist; deployed with a unit and individually assigned. Some couples were dating, some newlyweds, some had been married for decades. Some had no children, some newborns, some school age, and some college age. Some parents had more than one child in the services. A few had both a spouse and child deployed. Some spouses and parents had previous military service themselves and compared their expectations as a service member to that of a family member.

For some, this was their first deployment. Others had many years of military experience with numerous deployments and reunions. I talked with some families just before and after their homecoming, others a few months or a year into the reunion, and a few I followed for a year through their ups and downs. Some lived near a military base, others lived far away from anyone who understood military life. Some had great support and others felt completely isolated. A few were family readiness group leaders or ombudsmen, while some were not part of a support group at all. During the months following homecoming, some couples and individuals sought counseling or special support programs for common readjustment concerns, high stress or trauma, marriage counseling, separation anxiety, injuries, or grief.

In addition to men and women going through the reunion experience themselves, I also talked with chaplains, doctors, and therapists who had met with military families after a deployment. They summarized common concerns brought to them by service members and family members.

Some families had fairytale endings. Most worked hard to rebuild their families after much time and change. A few suffered great losses, including the death of a loved one.

Selected stories are used throughout the book as examples and inspiration for other military families going through similar aspects of homecoming and reunion. Though I wasn't able to share the story of every family I interviewed, each story was important because it helped shape the overall information and advice given.

Of all those I spoke with, the voices of the military wives and mothers were the strongest. In most cases, that person felt it was her responsibility to know how to help herself, her service member, and her family through the reunion experience. Family members I spoke with shared the feeling that military leaders would try to prepare their service member for reunion at some level, but the family may or may not receive the same support. Many fiancées, spouses living away from a unit base, and most parents whose children were deployed felt left out of the picture and on their own to find support and information. For these reasons, I chose to write the book with the partner and parent in mind as the primary audience.

Most of the book is organized chronologically by common event: the homecoming, adjusting to being together again, dealing with longer-term issues, and beginning the rest of your life. In "Introduction: The Answers," I summarize the top advice from families I interviewed and share ideas that work in both deployment and reunion as well as at any time in your life.

"Chapter One: Planning the Rendezvous" presents that wonderful homecoming event, the beginning of the honeymoon for many couples, and the great relief that your service member is home and safe. Military lingo often refers to reunion as the event of reuniting at homecoming and reintegration as the period of time following reunion. I have not been so formal here. The high of homecoming may last a few days or a few months. I refer to everything else as reunion, the being together again.

"Chapter Two: Learning to Dance Again" talks about those initial adjustments after your loved one comes home. Many service members and spouses say that the first few months hold the greatest stress and adjustments related to daily living. Common challenges include getting used to a change in environment and lifestyle, reestablishing intimacy and in-person communication, adjusting routines and decision-making, and rebuilding relation-ships after being apart for so long.

"Chapter Three: Stress and Other Things We Worry About" provides an overview of some of the post-deployment challenges that families sometimes face, such as anxiety, depression, and PTSD. Of course, there is no substitute for professional guidance and treatment. The intent of this chapter is to help answer questions that nearly everyone asked. How has this deployment changed my loved one? How will I know if something is wrong? What should I look for and expect? What should we do if we have concerns? Each circumstance is unique, but the stories others have shared may give you perspective and courage to know how to best help your own family.

"Chapter Four: Caregiving and Grief" reflects on the caregiver role you have had throughout the deployment and the everyday grief you may experience due to the changes in your life. This chapter is especially for anyone who has experienced a life-changing event during the deployment or reunion. For some families I talked with, this was the death of a young child. For some, it was welcoming home an injured service member. And, unfortunately, not everyone comes home. So for some, it was experiencing the ultimate sacrifice of the service member they loved. I hope these stories will help you if you find yourself in one of these situations.

"Chapter Five: Continuing the Journey" focuses on life after the first few months of reunion. Many families I talked with said they felt the first few months of reunion were very different from the fifth or sixth or twelfth month. Most of the families whose loved ones served for fifteen months or more, especially in dangerous assignments, said the time after the first three months was even more stressful because of longer-term decisions about relationships, careers, pending deployments, and individual challenges related to the deployment experience.

"Appendix: Resources for Your Happily Ever After" is meant to be a starting point for additional resources that may help you in your reunion. It lists books, Web sites, and programs that other military families say they have found helpful. Resources are changing and being added all the time, so I encourage you to please let other families know about resources that have helped you. You can go to www.lifeafterdeployment.com for an updated list and to submit your thoughts and recommendations.

My own personal story has changed since writing *Surviving Deployment: A guide for military families.* While I have many wonderful reunion stories to share from my husband's deployments as a Marine, I unfortunately now have broader experience that allows me to better understand the families in "Chapter Four: Caregiving and Grief." Bob came home safely from many types of deployment situations. Just when life had settled into our new normal and became less frightening, Bob was diagnosed with stage four colon cancer and died two years later. He is now on what I call the Ultimate Deployment. I don't know when we'll be together again but I hope that our reunion will be like the fairy tale we all dream about. One of the greatest sources of support for me has been my military family. I have truly felt the receiving end of the motto "taking care of our own." Thank you.

Thank you to each person who took the time to talk with me, send emails, and share your incredible stories for this book. I laughed and cried with you and so will so many others thanks to your willingness to allow us into your private lives. You didn't simply give us a picture of your homecoming hug, you gave us a glimpse into something much deeper. In the midst of being separated from someone you love, life continued on, with its births and deaths, house fires and hurricanes, and growing older. By sharing the pain and joy of the next chapter in your life, you have opened up hope and possibilities for others who are reuniting with their loved ones.

My best wishes to all military families. Thank you for your sacrifice. May each and every day bring you the joy of homecoming and a lifetime of love. God bless you.

—kmp

Introduction

The Answers

I've always liked it when hard puzzles give you the answers in the back. Since you're busy with deployment and reunion, I thought you might like to have all the answers up front!

Some of you will read this book a few months before homecoming while you are still separated from your loved one. That's wonderful because a healthy reunion begins while you are apart. Everything you do to end the deployment on a positive note—what you do to strengthen your relationship during the deployment and how well you communicate, respond to stress, and take care of yourself while apart— provides a great foundation for your family during reunion. So if you are reading this book during the deployment, use the tips in this section now. If you are in your reunion, many of the same things that brought you through deployment will also carry you in reunion. Use these tips to help you manage the changes and adjustments you are experiencing now that your loved one is home.

Lana Schmidtke (wife):

We live on a hobby farm in Lisbon, North Dakota. My husband, Dan, left for his fifteen-month deployment on one of the coldest days of the year. The girls and I went to see the convoy off and then they went to school and I went to work. I knew the quicker we got on with our life the better we would be. That evening we came home and did chores.

Well, the water had frozen in the chicken coop where we housed our geese, chickens, and ducks so instead of taking the time to thaw out the water I went to the garage and got a bucket for water to get them through the night. I watered those birds and called it a night.

The next morning, we set out to do the chores before tackling another day. Jordon and I went down to the barn while Dani went to the coop. As Jordon and I were doing the big animal chores, Dani came down to the barn with a huge warning to us, saying, "Don't anyone go into the chicken coop. There has been a MASS MURDER." Low and behold we went into the coop and every bird in there except one lone chicken was deader than a doorknob. Little did I know that the green bucket I chose to water the birds with was Dan's antifreeze bucket. I had fed the birds enough antifreeze along with their water to downsize the chores real fast.

Having nothing in the coop was one less building we had to go to each evening and morning so we learned to joke about the way mom downsized the chores on day one.

We did not share this story with Dan until he was home and wanted to go see all the animals. Finally, I had to confess to him about my way of dealing with too many chores. He thought we were nuts the way we all three of us began to giggle when he said, "Now let's go see the birds." He did not find the humor in it at first but now he loves to share that story as much as we do.

Laugh, Love, and Buy More Underwear

I have been asked many times what the three things are that would help anyone in a deployment or reunion. The answers I give are the three things I use as guiding principles at any time in my life:

1) As often as possible, laugh good hearty belly laughs.

2) See through eyes of love.

3) Buy more underwear.

Laugh Good Hearty Belly Laughs

We've all heard the phrase "laughter is the best medicine." Well, I believe that if we can still laugh—at ourselves, a situation, a joke—it will be okay. It feels good to laugh and it lightens our load considerably. While a good laugh may not solve a problem, it may give us a lighter perspective and calm our in-the-moment emotions to be able to deal with a problem or stressful situation.

One night my then-three-year-old son was really angry at dinner and in all seriousness he said, "Let's just sit here and cry about it." It caught me off guard and I started to laugh. That line was good for about three weeks. In any tense situation, we'd say that line and laugh.

Use your sense of humor. Can't think of anything to laugh at? There are plenty of good family movies that are so silly you can't help but laugh. Plan a family night where you have nothing to do but soak up the one-line jokes and kooky antics of a comedy rental.

This "lighten the moment" principle can be applied in many other ways, too. For example, when you crank up good dance music, it's hard not to dance. And when you are dancing, it's hard to be angry or frustrated or worried or depressed. Use whatever gives you and your family a positive way to bring up your spirits.

See Through Eyes of Love

It sounds simple to say that we should show our love to those we love most, but when we're emotional, angry, upset, stressed, impatient—all those things we tend to be from time to time during deployment and reunion—it's sometimes the ones we love most who get our worst.

Beth Johnson's two-year-old daughter, Emma, was sitting on the floor trying to undress a doll whose clothes fit too tightly. Each time Emma became frustrated with the doll, she reached over and hit Beth. "Emma didn't know how else to deal with her frustration, so she took it out on me!" Beth says. "I guess she somehow knows that the person she loves most is safe to hit because I'll love her anyway. And maybe I'll even eliminate her frustration by undressing the doll for her."

In some ways, we all act like that toddler, subconsciously feeling safe that we can take things out on loved ones. At a young age, we learn that forgiveness of love. However, during deployment and the adjustments of reunion, those types of reactions can be perceived as a lack of love and support. It's hard to live with someone else no matter how compatible you are. But you can find ways to remind yourself of your love for that person and ways you can respectfully deal with adjustments. Rather than react in hurtful ways, act in loving ways.

When Gina Netterson's husband came home, she bought him his own set of "everything from toothpaste to coffee cups." Before the deployment, they had argued over irritations like putting the cap on the toothpaste or cleaning the crud out of the bottom of the coffee mug. But during the deployment, she realized none of that really mattered.

Gina explains, "During his deployment, I looked at this picture of us together laughing. He's holding me and we're looking into each other's eyes. It's my favorite picture because neither of us had a care in the world except for each other. I decided that when he came home, I didn't want any of that other unimportant stuff getting in the way so I got him his own version of everything so he can do what he wants with it. There are still some things about living with another person—he's messy and I'm neat—that this plan doesn't take care of, but I just put that picture in my mind and remind myself how much I love him. Then I smile and let the little stuff fall away."

Watch and listen to yourself over the next few days as you interact with your family. Don't take them for granted. Express your love and appreciation. Use loving responses. Instead of yelling at your loved ones, give them a hug.

Whether you are dealing with your child's misbehavior or adjusting to the annoying habits you forgot your spouse had, make sure your first thought before you speak or act is how much you love this person. It will help you bring what's important to the surface and let the rest go.

Keep a picture of your loved one by your bedside. Make it a fun photo that reminds you of what you love about his or her personality or your relationship. It will be the first thing you wake up to and the last thing you see before you sleep, and it will be a reminder of your love. During reunion (and all your time together), take five minutes out of your day to remind each other of something you love about each other. The more you reinforce your friendship and love, the fewer petty comments about the toothpaste cap you'll have and the more you'll enjoy each other's company.

To remind yourself how much you love your kids, watch them sleep. Every night, before I go to bed, I watch my son sleep. He looks like an angel, so peaceful, and I fall in love all over again for the next day. Another idea is to keep a notebook or journal with little things your child says or does throughout the day that make you smile. Keep it in a common area such as your family room or kitchen so it's nearby and you can record just after the moment. Once a week or so read back through and remind yourself of all the reasons to smile.

Buy More Underwear (or kill the chickens)

The more underwear you have, the less often you need to do laundry. So get more underwear for yourself and everyone else in the family. You have more important ways to spend your time than doing laundry.

What this principle really means, of course, is to generally have less to do of the less important tasks so you can focus on time with each other.

You may end up doing this by accident, like Lana Schmidtke did when she killed the chickens on their hobby farm. Or you might need to take a look at your schedule, responsibilities, and personal time to make sure you have a good balance. We can all do everything—at a cost. Are you bored or feeling insane during this time? Are the things you are spending time on the best choices? Is this the best use of your talent? Are you spending time on what is most important to you?

Make Time for You

When you travel on an airplane, the flight attendant instructs you that if oxygen is needed during the flight, you should secure your own mask before assisting others. Yet during deployment most of us have a hard time taking care of ourselves first when there is so much else to do and worry about. And during reunion, we may feel guilty for spending time on ourselves instead of giving each moment to our loved ones.

What do you need to keep balance in your life and feel like you have energy to be a happy and healthy person for yourself and your loved ones? Most people need to be physically healthy, have a creative outlet or contribution, a source of inner strength such as faith in God or a higher meaning, and relationships with family and close friends. Upon further reflection, you might also discover you need chocolate, music, or something else you can get jazzed about. During deployment, find what keeps you in balance, encourage and help your family to keep their own balance, and keep those oxygen masks on during the sometimes bumpy ride through reunion. When your family is back together again, it can seem selfish to take time for yourself, but taking time to renew your own well being will give you more energy, a clearer mind, and much more patience as you contribute to your reunion.

Get the Basics

Don't underestimate the physical toll a deployment and reunion can have on you. Get the basics every day: exercise, sleep, and healthy food.

Exercise is often last on our list, but during high stress times, it is one of the things that helps us most. Schedule a time and place that works with your daily routine, style, and budget. Maybe you enjoy rowing on the river, walking with a friend, intense

---

Two Out of Three Rule

The goal is to exercise, get plenty of rest, and eat healthy foods every day. During this stressful time, make sure you get at least two out of three each day. Use these guidelines to help you determine how close you are to meeting this goal.

	Goal	Minimum to Count
Exercise	30-40 min. cardio/weights	20 min. (running after kids doesn't count)
Sleep	8 hours uninterrupted	7 hours 5 hours uninterrupted (naps count)
Food & Water	3 healthy meals 2 healthy snacks 10-12 glasses water	breakfast, healthy snacks (no vending machines) 4 glasses water

---

workouts with a trainer, yoga at the YMCA, or running up and down your basement stairs. Make it fun and worthwhile. Select two or three types of exercise you enjoy. If you need more incentive, reward yourself when you meet your goals. Keep it simple—just do it.

Ensure other members of your family get their exercise, too, but keep it separate from you if possible. Once in a while, it's nice to have a family bike ride or a canoe trip with your spouse. But running after little ones is not the same as running two miles on your own. And your older child will likely release more stress running hard in a soccer game. You might need to change your routines after the deployment if your family schedules change, but keep the commitment for all of you to get the exercise you each need.

Sleep can be hard to come by when you are anxious or worried or have a lot on your mind. Keep a bedtime routine and create a sleep environment. Don't watch TV in bed or eat late at night. Instead, take a warm, relaxing bath or stretch. Feel ready for the next day by making lunches or setting out clothes ahead of time. Keep a pad of paper and pen by your bed. Write out your worries to get them off your mind—you can deal with the list tomorrow. Go to bed when you're tired. Keep the rest of your family on a routine to wake up and go to sleep at the same time every day so you can all rest well at night.

Drink plenty of water, eat breakfast, and choose healthy snacks. If you make healthy food easy and accessible, you are more likely to choose it. Turn down a candy bar because you have a nutrition bar in your handbag or pocket. Keep almonds in your pantry and carrots and yogurt in the fridge. Carry a water bottle with you and fill it on the hour. Take a vitamin.

Use Your Creative Talents

Using your creativity to make something or to express yourself can help you balance your emotional energy. What creative outlets do you enjoy? Perhaps it's writing, photography, music, art, decorating, scrapbooking, gardening, or woodworking. One of the most common outlets is writing. Journaling is a great way to get things off your mind, capture how you feel about the day's events, and sort through hot emotions. It's interesting to look back at your writing six months later and see how your perspective has changed.

During reunion, some families plan simple creative time together, such as planting a garden or creating a family newsletter. It's important to continue to find some activities, though, that allow each person to feel that they are contributing unique talents and renewing their own creative energies through individual activities.

Sgt. Jack Gorder used woodworking to relax and get back into his home routine after spending eighteen months in Afghanistan.

"I needed to work with my hands and see the tangible results of something useful," he says. "I felt I was contributing so much overseas and when I first came home, I felt lost and kind of useless. So I got my tools out and made a bookshelf for my daughter and a sewing table for my mom. Not huge things, but practical. It helped me with my transition."

For Sharon Prince, writing poetry and songs became her way of expressing how she felt about the war in Iraq, her Marine son's injuries, and the changes she experienced in their family before and after his deployment. "I couldn't say these things outright, but writing the poems and songs let me feel out what was really in my heart and the end result was something I could share with my son and our family in a non-threatening way. I think in a way, my writing helped us all heal, and for me it was one way I could help myself come to terms with my son's injuries and feel I was doing something for him, for us."

Stacy Westbrook created a scrapbook about her husband's deployment. She still kept her usual family scrapbooks, but this one was special because "it's not about our life here—it's all about him and the deployment." She clipped articles and saved his letters and emails. She even included cards from memorials of troops from their base who died. "He loved this scrapbook," she says.

Renew Your Inner Strength

The saying "there are no atheists in foxholes" applies to the family at home, too. Helen Mayers said the one thing that got her through her son Danny's deployments was her faith and her church community. "You can't go through a deployment or reunion without faith. I can't imagine even trying," she says. "I spent my life protecting and worrying about my little child. And now I have nothing I can do but pray for him and trust that God will give me many more years that I can spoil Danny rotten!"

Whether it's faith in God or some higher meaning in life, you and your family need a source of strength that reaffirms everything will be okay, no matter what happens.

What is your source of faith? What guides you? What inspires you? What lifts your spirits when you are down or scared or sad or doubtful? Find quiet time to reflect and renew. Feed your soul. Pray for grace.

Barb Kraft, like many military family members, believes that God will get her family through whatever comes. Her four children picked up on her faith. She shares, "My kids prayed whenever they were afraid. There were many nights they were awake crying, afraid and missing their dad. I helped them to put their worries and cares at God's feet so they could just be kids. They really grew up spiritually because of this deployment. Kids are so tangible. It's an amazing thing to see your kids put faith in someone they can't see."

For Stacy Westbrook, going to church and keeping a strong faith in God is a good way to "check your worry." She advises, "You need to find people who support you 100%. There is a military spouse group at my church, led by a retired couple. The woman who leads it prays with me at church and calls me and hugs me."

"God speaks to my heart sometimes through other people around me," says Patricia Allender. "Some days I am looking for that faith. That ounce that will answer what comes next, how I'll keep working hard at this for our family. And then a song will come on the radio or a friend will call or even the grocery store clerk will say something silly that at that moment is so profound I just know it's encouragement from heaven. Be out among people so it's easier to get those messages!"

Surround Yourself with Positive, Supportive People

The right people around us can make all the difference during both deployment and reunion. A positive attitude, an inspirational outlook, and a good sense of humor can brighten our day and perspective. Also, having people who care about us contact us regularly helps us recognize any potentially harmful behaviors or symptoms.

"I wouldn't have made it without my sister's weekly phone call," says Adison Browne. "She is so positive about life. She always had a funny story or an interesting insight to share about her week. She helped me laugh."

Noelle McCarthy appreciated her neighbor Bethany's visits. "She made a point of stopping by. She was very direct with me, asking when was the last time I had been to a doctor, inviting me to walk with her to make sure I was exercising. It was nice to know that someone was noticing and cared enough to ask about the practical things."

But sometimes you need to evaluate whether the people around you are really supporting you. Wanda Remalling found that her normal Tuesday lunch gatherings with friends turned sour during her son's deployments. "They talked about the war in a negative way as if I weren't even there. And their opinions made it sound like my son was an animal for carrying a weapon. I had no idea they were like this," she says.

Jean Denney was dealing with her own depression during her fiancé's deployment when a welcomed old friend stopped by. "Three weeks before Reece was coming home, a friend I had met before I knew Reece came into town. He started to hang out with me and my kids. But when he said he had other feelings for me, I ended the friendship," she says. "It's a big toll on the guys to worry about home. Don't cheat on them. Their job is hard enough and it makes it easier to know that everything with you and at home is okay. I waited until Reece got home to tell him about it. He thanked me for waiting for him and staying faithful."

Amy Granger says she had a hard time talking with her mother-in-law during the deployment: "She was always negative and frightened. Every time we talked, I had to try to calm her down. She watched news all the time and was worried John would die and she constantly got my blood pressure up instead of making me feel like it would be okay." Though Amy realized that the conversations might be helping her mother-in-law, they were completely draining her. "So I set her up to receive the same newsletters and calls I did so we didn't have to talk so often," Amy says. "I felt so bad and guilty but it wasn't helping me at all to feel the way I did when she called."

Maintain Social Relationships

We all have different needs for relationships and social activities. Some like social gatherings such as bunko or a soup night with friends. Others like to be active in sports, as a player or coach, or to contribute their talents in a church group or choir or volunteer organization. Some like intellectually stimulating gatherings such as a writers group or book club. And then there are always quiet lunches with friends, coffee with neighbors, or a night out at a comedy club or theater performance.

Whatever works for you socially, you need to be around people outside your immediate family. It gives you perspective, energy, and someone else to care about how you are doing. It gives you a sense of being part of a large community and can remind you that there is more going on than this deployment. And during reunion, while you want to spend as much time as possible with your returned loved one, keeping some level of outside social connection can help you maintain perspective.

Make it easy to be with other people. Take an afternoon to get to know a line up of babysitters (paid or volunteer) so you have choices and flexibility. Arrange for rides or equipment or whatever you might need to participate with a group or event. Get rid of the guilt—you need this!

Help Your Whole Being

Often during a deployment or reunion, a person hurts but can't quite describe the hurt. It might be physical or emotional. It might be an overwhelming feeling that's hard to pinpoint. I find it helpful to separate things into two categories, those aspects that reflect who I am as a person, and those aspects that reflect all the logistical chaos and responsibilities around me. For the "who I am" portion, consider reflecting on the Whole Person Wheel on the next page. For the logistical challenges in your life, which seem to throw this wheel out of kilter during deployment and reunion, considering getting a Mother Hen (more about that later in this chapter).

A Whole You

Each day, we make choices that affect different aspects of our well-being. To keep ourselves in balance, we need to pay attention to our health in each area of our whole being. The Whole Person Wheel on the following page is one way to think about and assess your health in different areas. Reflect on your commitment to nourish each area every day and to make choices that reflect your values.

When you make time to care for yourself in each area, the wheel turns smoothly. When any one area is lacking or pulling, you feel out of balance. What areas need nourishment for you to feel in balance? What commitments can you make that reflect your values in each area? Do you feel that your choices reflect your true self?

Abby Sobaski cautions military spouses to maintain their sense of self. "Don't get so wrapped up in what your spouse does. I want to be Abby, a nurse, not just Bryan's wife. You can lose yourself if you get too absorbed in the military and that's all it's about."

This is an opportunity for you to reflect on your true self and to plan simple ways to balance your physical, emotional, spiritual, intellectual, relational, and logistical needs even in the midst of a chaotic military lifestyle.

Out of Balance

The downside of not taking care of yourself can be very serious. Beyond getting more frequent colds or being irritable or lacking patience, you could become depressed or unable to care for yourself and others.

When Kara Kitchen-Glodgett's husband Forest deployed to Afghanistan for a year, she says, "It was like the movie *Ground Hog Day*, waking up and having the same day over and over again

Whole Person Wheel

Self Assessment

Take a moment to reflect on each area of the wheel. What is going well? Are there areas in which you feel especially stressed? When one area is suffering or neglected, it affects other areas and you feel out of balance. Using a pencil, shade each section according to how you feel:

- Shade up to the first line from the center if you can express your goals and values in this area.
- Shade up to the second line if you do something each day to nurture this aspect of your life.
- Shade the whole section if you consistently meet your goals and your daily habits reflect your values.

Now look at the wheel as a whole. Are there areas of strength (completely shaded) that can help you nurture other areas?

Simple Action Plans

You don't need to commit to a complex, formal plan in order to see great improvements in your overall well being. Simply make a short list for yourself of three or four things you will do each day and general principles you will follow that help you meet your goals in each area. Hang a note on your mirror, computer, refrigerator, or other common area to remind yourself of the little ways you can make a big difference in keeping the whole you in balance. For example:

in a blur of day-to-day survival." She became depressed and didn't realize it. "You need to be well, especially for your kids," she says. "Looking back, I should have hired a babysitter once a week for a break and maybe that would have helped my son, Wyatt, too. He has extreme separation anxiety. I was on call 24x7 as a single parent. You need to give yourself permission to ask for help and take care of yourself."

Four months after Nina Hamilton's husband Trevar deployed to Iraq, she went to the doctor because she was feeling tired. "I didn't care about anything anymore. My daughter Mikaela was having a hard time in day care and I felt like I wasn't being a good parent." Her doctor put her on depression medication and told her the next month could be worse. A nearby National Guard family helped her out by taking Mikaela for a few hours at a time each week. One night, Nina overdosed on her pills. A friend tried to get her to go to the hospital but Nina refused because she works there. Her friend stayed the night to make sure she was okay. "That was a really tough time to get through. I'm so lucky I had friends and family around who cared," says Nina. Her brother moved in with her later in the deployment.

When Holly Burkin's son was injured in Iraq, she started drinking wine. "First it was a glass to relax myself in the evening. I was worried about him coming home. Then it became several glasses a day." By the time her son was released to their care, Holly was rarely sober. "It was the absolute worst way I could have handled my fear and grief. He needed my help with his therapy." With the encouragement of a few close friends at her church, Holly joined a support group and is now actively involved in her son's recovery.

Take Charge

You are in charge of so many things throughout your day, especially with added responsibilities and worry of the deployment and the stress of reintegrating responsibilities and decisions during reunion (which often takes more effort, time, and emotion than doing it yourself). Take control of what impacts you most.

Leave work at work. Say no to extra activities, such as volunteer work, unless it feeds your soul. When my son was having separation anxiety and I was feeling overwhelmed, our family therapist told me to leave work at 4 p.m. each day. I didn't think it was possible, but I told my team it was doctor's orders. I focused on the most important priorities and communicating progress with our team when I was at work. Then I left work at work and focused on home starting at four. It really helped. Now I have a different job with shorter, more flexible hours and it has really helped me and my family stay in balance.

A Mother Hen
(How to get all the help you need with just one phone call!)

I have a tough time asking for help. I wake up each morning with such optimism, thinking today is the day I will be super woman! And it's usually not until my house is a wreck, lightning has struck, and at least five major appliances are broken that I hang my distress flag and hope a neighbor notices me crying when I take out the garbage. I have had to learn more about the concept of help.

When my husband was sick with cancer, people said to me, "If you ever need anything, let me know." That was overwhelming. Usually when I needed something, it was last minute, unplanned, and I had no idea which of those kind people to call. Did they mean if I needed last-minute babysitting for a sick child? Did it mean I could call at 9 p.m. because I just realized we're out of milk? Would it be too much to ask them to just shovel the snow or mow the lawn indefinitely whenever it needed to be done?

Then one day I met a woman had been through a similar situation. She shared a wonderful idea about how to manage all those kind offers of help. I talked with my friend Linda and then asked everyone to let Linda know how they could help. People were honest with her about what they could do. Some signed up for the last-minute babysitting, others to run errands. (I sent her my Target list.) One said, "I don't babysit, but I can fix anything."

Whenever I needed something, I called or emailed Linda. She called someone on her list. Three years later, I still have people from that list helping me, even though it's still hard to ask.

So, maybe you need a Linda, or Chief Helper, or Mother Hen. Here is how it works:

Make a list of all the things you wish you didn't have to do yourself. Maybe during a deployment, your list includes mowing the lawn, getting groceries, and finding last minute babysitters. Maybe during your reunion, your list includes things you wish you didn't still have to take care of but that your returning loved one isn't ready to take over doing.

Sometimes it's hard to accept help that's offered.

In Heather Greene Hinckley's town in Vermont, people have a hard time accepting help. "They are proud and won't take handouts," she says. Heather encourages people to think of it a different way, though. It's not so much that they are helping you as you are letting them do something to contribute. "You have to realize that people don't do it because they feel sorry for you," Heather says. "They do it because they support our troops, they want to show patriotism, want to make it easier for you and do their part in thanks for what you and your loved one are doing."

Sometimes it's the wrong kind of help.

Susan Gillson's husband, Glen, spent seven years away from their family. He moved from reserve to active duty reserve status and first was stationed two hours away. Since the duration was unknown, they didn't move their family. They saw him on weekends for what turned out to be three years. Then he spent two and a half years at various stateside

Now think of a good friend, neighbor, or family member who has asked how they can help. Choose someone who is organized. Ask that person to be your Mother Hen.

Your Mother Hen takes your list and assigns someone to do each task on the list. Whenever anyone asks what they can do to help you, tell them to contact Mother Hen.

Usually we stop ourselves from asking for help because we think we should do it all ourselves, or we think someone else expects us to do it all ourselves, or we feel bad asking as though we are placing a burden on someone else.

---

locations such as Missouri and Alaska, while the family remained in Minnesota. Then he deployed to Afghanistan for one and a half years.

One of the biggest challenges for Susan was people in her community not understanding military life. "They try to be helpful, but they don't get it," she said. When Glen deployed to Afghanistan, her church decided she needed help. "So they sent a person to meet with me once a week to make sure I was okay. What I needed was someone who knew about car repair—real stuff. I had just spent five and a half years away from my husband. I knew how to handle the separation. It's the daily life stuff like fixing things that I needed help with. Hey, if someone wants to come fix my car, I'll take that kind of help!"

Deanna Wellsted advises, "The deployment is a long time. The community goes away after a while. It's easy for them to forget, but you are living it. They haven't really forgotten, but they don't know what you need. You can tell them." And then after the deployment, you especially need to tell them what you need because they might think everything is taken care of when it isn't.

By using a Mother Hen, you have only one person to tell what you need. Your Mother Hen won't mind asking others because it's to help someone else: you. And the people your Mother Hen asks will only say yes if they really want to. They won't feel bad telling Mother Hen no.

If you still feel uncomfortable asking for help or accepting help, remember that what comes around goes around. My mom lives near Fort Drum, New York. During each major deployment, she "adopts" a family. She usually meets them at church, often when the mom is struggling with three or four little ones in the pews. When Cassie's husband was in Afghanistan, my mom became like a second mom to her and like a grandmother to her four children. One day Cassie said to her, "How can I ever repay you?" My mom told her that she appreciated what all of my neighbors were doing to help me in Minnesota when she couldn't be there. So this was her way of repaying their kindness. "Someday," she told Cassie, "you'll pass it on to someone else."

Maintain Strong Relationships

Communicate

Communication is the number one thing families say keeps them together during deployment and makes reunion transitions easier. Letters, love notes, phone calls, email, care packages, whatever type of communication works best for you, do it frequently and make it part of your daily life. And then maintain that time to communicate when you are together again.

Many parents whose adult children deployed say they grew closer to their child through the deployment communication. This was true for Gary Peters and his son Jonathan. "He could ask me the hard questions in a letter," Gary says. "He shared things he couldn't say in person about his work in Iraq and told me how proud he wanted me to be. I couldn't be any prouder."

Heidi Thatcher cherished the letters she received from her deployed son, Gene, and talked with her daughter-in-law every day by phone. "I gained respect for how my son cared for his family and what a great mom my daughter-in-law Katie is. Katie and I have remained close now that Gene is home."

Intimacy

One of the toughest changes going through deployment and reunion is intimacy. "You get used to being able to touch him and share your feelings and then you shut down during deployment," says Rian Saint James. "It's so hard to find a substitute for that closeness. And then when he comes home it is this awkward time before we open back up. I don't mean the sex, but the closeness."

Amidst the stress of a spouse's deployment and reunion, you might be tempted to try to recreate that intimacy with others. Choose appropriate relationships that support, encourage, and strengthen your marriage. And shower your affection and love on kids, pets, and plants.

"Make a commitment to the relationship or get out of it," says Abby Sobaski. "Don't put yourself in situations that tempt you. Keep the same level of respect as if your partner were gone overnight. Otherwise, it's a cop out. I didn't need my husband to hear that I was out dancing with other men at a bar. Neither of us needs that stress."

Parents whose children are deployed also miss intimacy. Heidi Thatcher says, "I wanted so much to hug Gene. He's still my little boy, you know. I want to protect him and make sure he knows how loved he is." She suggests that parents find ways to be with young children, such as spending time with grandchildren or volunteering through local church or school programs. Adopting pets or tending a garden also help, she says. Jarrod Gruber volunteered in a hospital wing "delivering movies, magazines, and smiles. It was my way of feeling like I was caring for someone in a concrete way," he says.

Writing letters each day to your loved one also helps. When you write 300 letters to someone in a year, you can't help but share intimate thoughts and grow closer.

Support Children

During deployment and reunion, your children have many of the same fears, anxieties, emotions, and needs that you do, but they understand it all even less. They need you, through your example, love, attention, direct support, and guidance, to help them stay healthy and find ways to live happily during this challenging time.

Basics

Kids need the same basics you do: exercise, sleep, healthy food. In fact, it's even more important that kids get all three every day because they don't know how to adjust when they don't get enough. Next time your child acts up, first ask yourself if he or she has had enough exercise, sleep, and nutritious food that day.

Make healthy snacks readily available—fresh fruit in a bowl on the table; veggies cut up in the fridge; peanuts, cheese, and other bite-size protein snacks.

Active lifestyles help relieve stress naturally. Make sure kids get outside, whether that means participating in competitive sports or riding bikes with friends. Balance active time with quiet time. All kids need both physical and creative outlets. Interests in music, theater, poetry, or simply reading a good book help exercise their minds and stimulate creative thought and expression. Keeping a journal is a great way for kids to process some of their energy and emotions.

One of the best ways to support your children during the unstable time of deployment and reunion is to create as much predictability as possible. Establish routines. Routines help kids understand what is expected and what to expect. Routines help their bodies know when to eat and sleep and run. Have a menu and a set time for dinner. Help them go to bed at the same time each day. It helps their bodies naturally wind down and get good restful sleep. Also keep in mind that routine for kids is as much about the order of things as it is about time. My son's bedtime routine, for example, is to put on jammies, then have a snack, then brush teeth, then read a book, then go to sleep—in that order. We try to begin the routine at 7:30 each evening so he is in bed by 8:00. But if an activity takes us to 8:00, he still needs to follow the order of things to feel ready to go to sleep. We can't skip snack just because bedtime is later.

Boundaries

A friend of mine who lives on a farm says "kids are like cows." Cows go out each morning and walk to the fence. They want the fence to be there; it confirms that their world is still as they know it. Then they come back to the fields and go about their day.

No matter how much they test them, children and teens also like to have boundaries. Build a fair pasture and tell them where the fence is. Provide a framework and then be patient and flexible so you can adapt within that framework. Know that they'll test you, but don't confuse walking to the fence with not wanting a fence. To them, everything in their world changed when their parent deployed. And everything changes again when that parent returns. They'll feel more secure when you expect them to honor rules and keep their lives in order.

Be predictable and consistent, with logical consequences. Your kids count on you to respond consistently when things don't go as planned or when they misbehave. You build trust and give them confidence when they know how you will respond.

Remember that you are also under a great deal of stress. When your kids act up, take a look at your own behavior. Are you in control of your own emotions at that time? Is your response appropriate for their action or would a little more patience or a sense of humor better resolve the situation?

Help them understand what's appropriate, what's negotiable and not. My son and I have a rule: If he disagrees, he's not allowed to whine, but he can say "Mom, I disagree" and state his position for me to consider.

Don't assume your kids have the same view you do of what is right or wrong. Be clear so they are clear.

Control

Children have little control over their environment and most of the time feel they have no say in anything. During a deployment, they have a heightened awareness that they can't control world events and the dangerous situations their deployed parent may be in. They had no control over their parent leaving for the deployment and no say in when their parent will return home. They may resent changes that affect them and have mixed emotions about the future. There are several ways you can help them feel more in control. Whenever possible, give them a choice. They can help plan a menu, have a say in rewards or consequences for broken rules (they will often come up with stricter guidelines than you might), or choose from a short list of fun activities. In addition to helping them feel more in control, letting them participate in appropriate decisions helps them develop problem-solving and leadership skills.

Explain directions. If they know the steps, they'll be more confident in the outcome. Plan ahead. Kids often act out when they are stressed, in a rush, or surprised. Allow extra time to get to places so you are all less stressed when you get there.

Feeling Safe

You will all worry about your service member's safety, especially if there have been injuries or deaths close to you. Remind your children of all the specialized training and equipment that helps keep the parent safe. Check with your local base about a family day where children could see the safety equipment the unit uses. Help your children understand that what is reported by the media does not necessarily depict the situation that your loved one is in. Encourage them to ask you questions directly; keep your answers honest and age appropriate. Without real information, children may make it up themselves.

With worldwide real-time news coverage ever-present, it's easy for kids to apply far-away dangers to home and worry that something bad will happen to their family, too. This isn't limited to thoughts of terrorism or "bad guys." They may worry about a fire, car accident, or natural disaster. To help alleviate these fears, have a safety plan and practice it.

With one parent who has been gone, younger children especially may fear you will go away, too. When you go out, tell them when you'll be home, and don't be late. Don't threaten to leave them when they misbehave. Tell your kids that you like being with them. When you are with them, be present; pay attention to them. During reunion, you may find that kids won't trust that their parent is really home. They want proof each day that their parent is staying for a while.

Kids may also fear the death of either parent or what will happen to them if that happens. My son once asked me, "What will happen to me if you die?" It turns out what he really wanted to know was who would pick him up from school and how would they know to do that. Once he understood the plan, he didn't worry so much about me dying. Whenever he was especially clingy, I reminded myself that he wasn't trying to annoy me, he was either afraid something would happen to me or needed to know what comes next if something bad did happen.

Many families caution that the fears of deployment don't really go away during reunion. You still worry about each other's safety. You know how precious it is to be together.

Tangibles

Younger children, especially, need reminders they can see and touch. During deployment and reunion, think of ways to actively connect the deployed parent and each child in tangible ways.

Kara Kitchen-Glodgett's family readiness group held a craft night and made pillowcases with an ironed-on photo of their soldier for each child in the unit. Her son Wyatt slept with his "daddy pillow" every night. Her toddler, Kade, used it as a "daddy bag" and carried his favorite toys and stuffed animals in it.

Joe Schmidt hung two clocks in his kitchen, one with the local time and one with Mom's time in Germany. His five children always knew what time it was where their mom was working at the hospital. The clock gave the five-year-olds, especially, a reference point. At meal times, they guessed what she was doing at that time during her day over there.

A tangible expressive outlet can give a child a special voice during deployment and help the child remember and share events and feelings with a returning parent. Encourage your child to write in a journal or keep a scrapbook. This can be a simple notebook or photo album, an elaborate multimedia project, or a deployment-specific journal such as Rachel Robertson's *Deployment Journal for Kids*.

During reunion, continue to find tangible ways to connect, such as designated parent-child activities, one-on-one conversations, or notes slipped into a lunchbox or pocket.

Bill Church shares, "My daughter was fifteen and my son was nine when I came home. I had missed a lot and was determined to get that real connection back. I took my daughter to a concert and went with my son to Cub Scout camp. We played ball in the back yard. I showed them pictures and letters I had kept and asked about their friends and classes at school. Anything to let them know I was interested. You have to make the time and get in their world."

Ann Grados wrote a book with her son. "We started with our homecoming and we each wrote about what it was like being together again. Every Saturday, we wrote a new chapter with a story about something that happened that week. It helped make the things we missed less important and helped us focus on our new memories. We did this for two months and then wrote a happy ending: 'Luke and his mom had many more adventures—maybe you'll read about those in another book some day!' He loves to show everyone that book."

Heroes

Kids need strong role models. You are your child's greatest opportunity for a role model during a deployment and reunion.

You can show kids by your actions how to positively deal with stress and the unexpected.

Give children opportunities to interact with other adults, such as a coach, teacher, chaplain, or neighbor.

Keep them involved so they have good peer support. In your support network, are there children the same age who also have a parent deployed or recently returned? Are there some activities that have nothing to do with the military?

Choose modern-day heroes that offer your kids coping ideas and ways to look at life positively even when things look bleak. For a five-year-old boy, you might ask how Billy Blazes would deal with his fear. A fifteen-year-old girl might think about what keeps Ann Bancroft going when she's trekking across the Arctic.

A CEO I once worked for told me about his heavy travel schedule when his kids were growing up. "My wife could have made me the bad guy," he said. "Instead, she made me the hero. I've always appreciated that." Celebrate the deployed parent as a hero—because it's true!

Kids are heroes, too. Zachary Hinckley, age six, had a tough start to the school year while his dad was deployed. A classmate said, "Your dad is overseas killing kids like us." Zachary responded, "No he's not, he's a hero fighting so you can say that."

Celebrate your patriotism and the wonderful aspects of military service so you and your kids have plenty of reasons to feel really proud of your service member and yourselves.

Something to Believe In

As children mature, their belief structure changes. Fairy tales and magic tricks eventually give way to logic and laws of physics. Help children learn how to keep the faith as their world changes.

Share your spiritual or religious beliefs and life principles. Show them how you pray and how you find strength in your faith. Help them find their own sources of inner strength.

Young children believe in "happily ever after." Provide real-life examples for all ages so your kids can develop their own sense of what happiness is and different ways to think about a happy ending.

Consider a family ritual that helps keep your spirits up when you're down. Our family puts on loud music and dances together in the living room. It's hard to feel sad with great music playing and your family dancing and laughing.

Stress-Free Time

Sometimes kids just need to be kids. They already have so much stress—peer pressure, changing bodies, new things to learn. Military kids also have frequent moves, making new friends at new schools, and often living with a parent who is also stressed with single parenthood and other demands of a deployment.

Take time to do fun things. Plan special family times—pizza and movies on Friday night, bike rides on a Saturday, a trip to a local park or zoo. Make time for each child to have your individual attention.

Let your kids be messy, play, fool around, be silly, hang out, run wild in the back yard. They learn and express themselves better when they can experience their world at their own pace, in their own way. Not everything has to be right or perfect.

Tell jokes and stories. Laugh together. Showing your kids how to laugh when you want to cry is a wonderful life-long gift. Find ways to laugh at the situation, even if it means laughing at yourself.

Give kids an out when things aren't going well. Not everything has to be serious. Sometimes your sense of humor instead of quick punishment will make you all feel better.

Hug!

Build a unique relationship with each child. Take advantage of the little magical moments of the day to strengthen that relationship: enjoy a sunset or snowfall or rainbow, play in the rain, listen to their stories, look for bugs together, find a penny. Remember that not everything is about the deployment or reunion and it's not gloom; it's concentrated life!

Positive Life Lessons

As tough as it is to be separated from a parent, a deployment can be an incredibly positive experience for children. By watching their parents' actions during the deployment and reunion, kids learn amazing life lessons that will get them through any challenges they face in the future:

- You can love someone with all your heart even when you're apart.
- Friends and neighbors help us when we're facing tough challenges.
- A sense of humor and a good dose of faith can get us through really tough days.

The Mega Answer List

When I interviewed families, I asked them to contribute to a List of Things To Do and a List of Things Not To Do during reunion. In their own words, here is the advice these military families shared:

Things To Do:

- Communicate. Talk about your expectations—how you see the arrival, first day, first two weeks, what you each want it to be like. Decide together who should be at the homecoming and who you want to spend time with right away.
- Communicate some more. Take turns listening even if you don't like what the other person has to say.
- Communicate with your silence, your body language, your smile, your eyes, your loving hug, your acceptance, your patience, your love notes, your being there. Cry, laugh, talk, share, take walks, go grocery shopping together.
- Keep homecoming simple. All you really want is each other, so focus on that. Enjoy the magic of being

together again. If you both decide you want something
more elaborate, have someone else do the planning and
hosting and cleanup and thank yous. Don't overschedule
the first days after homecoming.

- Expect the unexpected.
- Involve children in planning—make signs, a countdown
  calendar, dinner plans, etc. Being part of it is good
  therapy on its own.
- Make life as stress-free as possible. Make meals ahead or
  arrange for friends to cook and deliver. Put things in
  order in other areas of your life.
- Be selfish with your time for each other. Include only
  those closest to you in the first few days. Create a new
  family time, such as a weekly family hour, when you all
  commit to being together without outside hassles. Plan
  time alone to help yourself reflect and gather your
  thoughts and energy, time as a couple, time with parents,
  time with each child and person who is close to you.
  Couples: Go on a date.
- Allow each person time to adjust. Give the service
  member space and time to rest and recuperate and
  adjust to being home. Be patient with family members
  as they adjust to having the service member back in
  their daily lives.
- Allow yourselves time to live separate lives as well, to
  spend time with your own friends and support systems.
- Help kids connect through the things that are important
  in their lives (school papers, games, etc.). Let kids have a
  voice, even if it's to say "I hate you."
- Stock the refrigerator with favorite foods.
- Get help, even if you didn't have it during deployment.
  Friends and neighbors can help make or freeze meals,
  fix things, or help with the house or kids. They are
  happy to be able to do something, so accept the help and

focus on your family. There is no time limit to asking for or accepting help.

- Spouses/fiancées: Get a cute outfit to wear to the homecoming.

- Follow your nesting instincts. Have a friend help you clean the house and put things in order. Will your service member notice? Not if he or she has been living in dusty tents! But it's a nice environment to be in and feels less stressful.

- Agree on a budget. Lots of people like to spend money after a deployment. Be sure you can afford it so it doesn't cause additional stress.

- Remember that you both have the same goal: to make it through deployment and have a happy reunion and life together.

- Allow yourself room for disappointment.

- Remember that it is common for people to overreact as they adjust to being together after a separation. Take a moment to think about how the other person might be feeling before you speak or react to things.

- Service member: Make a conscious effort to look for and comment on positive changes you notice, such as how your children have grown, new skills they have learned, household improvements. Tell family members you are proud of them. Show your appreciation for the extra work your spouse took on while you were away. Your family made good choices and decisions in your absence—respect that even if it's not how you would have handled it or you don't agree with the choices.

- Make the best out of the situation you have.

- Tell each other you want to be together, you love each other and you are needed.

- Find out what benefits you are entitled to after deployment. Talk about changes in pay, insurance, etc.

- Surround yourself with positive influences. If you're married, hang out with happily married people. If you're single, find friends who are confident and kind, who make good decisions and get along with their parents. If you're a parent, be around other parents who communicate well and have great relationships with their families. This reinforces all the good things you want for yourself and your family instead of dragging you down.

- Go to church. Walk in the woods. Do what helps you find peaceful moments.

- See it from the other person's point of view.

- Rekindle the friendship and romantic aspects of your relationship, and sort out the responsibilities afterwards. Talk about what responsibilities you would each like for the service member to take back.

- Take it one day at a time. You have each grown in ways that most couples and families never experience when living their daily lives together.

- Remember that there is a purpose for everything, even if we don't know it in this lifetime.

- Appreciate what you have. Don't take anything for granted.

- Be flexible. Be patient.

- Talk to other people who have been through this.

- Believe that if you can make it through this, you can make it through anything.

Things Not To Do:
- Don't expect homecoming to be perfect. It's not a movie.
- Don't expect life to be like it was before. Each of you and your lives together have changed during this deployment. And each reunion is different, too.
- Don't make plans for each other. Decide together.

- Don't make it all about you. It's bigger than that.
- Don't expect past issues to be resolved. You'll still need to work through them.
- Don't plan elaborate gatherings for the first few weeks of homecoming.
- Don't dwell on the little things that are likely to go wrong.
- Don't be in a hurry. Slow down and enjoy each moment together.
- Don't push the service member to talk about the deployment experience, especially if the circumstances were dangerous or upsetting. Some things the service member will tell you right away, others in time, and some things he will only be able to talk about with those who were there with him.
- Don't get overwhelmed by all the family readiness group information coming all at once.
- Don't beat yourself up if you've screwed up finances or some other issue during the deployment. Get advice and put a plan in action to fix it and move on.
- Don't throw a million projects on the list right away.
- Don't watch a lot of TV. Get some distance from the news so you can separate yourself from deployment activities and just exist with each other.
- Don't compare yourself to others. It's not a competition.
- Don't blame your service member for being gone.
- Don't argue about who had it worse.
- Service member: Don't just walk in and take charge. Don't criticize decisions. Don't jump to conclusions or make quick changes. Understand your new situation and discuss with your family first.
- Don't let things build up. Deal with it. Don't go to bed angry.

- Don't take it personally.
- Don't assume you know what the other person is thinking.
- Don't try to make up what you missed, just go on to the future together.
- Don't always listen to advice. It's your life together. Do what's right for you.

Whether you are reading this section a few months before your reunion or during your reunion, you'll find that much of the advice from these families works at any time in your life. If we take care of ourselves, focus only on the important stuff, communicate, act with love, and have faith and a sense of humor, we'll help each other get through whatever else comes.

Chapter One

Planning the Rendezvous

Homecoming. For some it is a fairy tale ending, a dream. For many, it is the first step in a long journey. It's the day we've been longing for and when it comes, it can bring with it the butterflies of a wedding day or the anxiety of going to a party with people you barely know. It's the relief of seeing someone safe whom you've worried about and prayed for every day. It is a new beginning.

Anissa Mersiowsky (wife):
   The house was ready, the banners were up, and we just waited for his return. Of course, as you probably know it was hurry up and wait. They delayed their arrival a couple times but it didn't matter at this point. We knew he was in Kuwait, safe and sound and waiting to see us. I remember the day so clearly. I had bought Kaitlyn a "my daddy's coming home" dress about nine months before, but it was probably the coldest March day Texas ever had. I scrambled to get her another outfit the day before he came home. We both had to bundle up, hats, gloves, the works. I was a little disappointed because I was so excited for her to wear her new dress, but again nothing really mattered because he was coming home.
   We met some friends and went to the parade field where they were going to come and we waited and waited and waited some more. It was such a long wait, especially with all the excitement. Luckily I brought Kaitlyn's stroller and some blankets because she ended up falling asleep all warm and

toasty in her stroller covered in a big warm blanket. She must
have been exhausted because when they arrived they had a
band playing and speakers blaring but she didn't wake up. In
fact, when they arrived I couldn't find Jeff because I couldn't
maneuver her stroller through the crowd. There were so
many familiar faces. I kept seeing friend after friend finding
her husband but I couldn't find Jeff. My neighbor found me
and said, "Go find him. I'll watch Kaitlyn." So I did, but still
through the thousands I could not find him. I remember
someone saying to me, "He's over there!" I went the way she
pointed and I saw him standing there. I'm crying even
describing this moment. He was home and safe and he
looked beautiful. It was almost a year ago but I remember it
vividly. The first thing he said to me was, "Where's Kaitlyn?" I
led him over to her and there she was, sleeping so peacefully
in this huge crowd of people. We hugged and kissed and just
stood there. It was surreal.

Barb Kraft (wife):

Our homecoming was not what I expected. A thousand
family members waiting for soldiers. Jerry's flight had been
delayed. I kept looking for him through the crowd, carrying
and leading our four kids. After thirty minutes of frustrated
searching in the cold, Jerry called on my cell phone. He was out
front with his mom. She got to see him before me. I don't have
a good relationship with my in-laws and things had escalated
during the deployment. So it was a big thing for me to say I
was okay with her coming. It was so hard. We went home and
spent time with just us and the kids for a couple weeks.

Tony Cerro (airman):

We rode up to the hangar and I was so nervous. I knew
my wife would be there with our three kids. I was sure our
littlest, who is three, wouldn't remember me. I was walking
toward the crowd, almost to the rope line when all of a
sudden, Carina broke free from my wife's arm and ran to me

as fast as her little legs would take her. I scooped her up and she nestled her face right into my neck and said, "Daddy, why did it take you so long to land that plane?" I laughed and thought my heart was going to burst right there. Carina didn't let go of me the whole time as I hugged my wife and two sons. All three kids were all over me at home that first day, telling me everything they could think of about who said what at school and the color of the drapes in their bedrooms and any other little thing they thought I missed out on. I didn't get to say two words to my wife until they went to bed. We just swapped these dumb little grins that said "I love you" over the commotion. It was the most wonderful, exhausting homecoming I've ever had. When we went to bed, my wife, Marietta, nestled in beside me in the same way Carina had. I didn't move all night. I just held her tight and slept like a baby. It was so good to be home.

Heather Greene Hinckley (wife):

I checked into the hotel a few days early to relax and set up some special things for him in the area. He sent me a rose every hour with a message on it. By the time he got off the plane, I had received six dozen roses—a dozen for each year we'd been together.

Kara Kitchen-Glodgett (wife):

Seeing him get off the plane, my knees were weak and I was crying hysterically. I looked at Wyatt (age six) and realized how strong we were trying to be. We ran out and jumped on Forest, crying and sobbing out of control. Kade (eighteen months) had a look on his face of no recognition and wanted to know "Who's got my mama?" Then Forest made a sound—a whistle—that he did when Kade was a baby. Kade recognized it. It was an amazing, wonderful moment. The next morning Kade ran around saying "dadda dadda dada."

I woke up the next morning and looked over. I thought I was dreaming, but Forest was really home.

Thea Testa (mom):

It seemed to take years as we waited at Fort Dix for the plane to land. While standing outside talking with one of the other mothers I became friends with over the eighteen months, we saw a plane fly over low with the word *World* on it. All we could do is look and say "Is it them? Is it them?" We both had our only child coming home. It was the best day of my life. Word came that their plane had landed. That is when tears started to flow. My stomach was in knots, so many emotions starting to surface. Knowing my son's feet were on American soil was the day I could have peace again. It was about an hour later that the buses pulled up front and one by one they handed their weapons over and walked into the hall to applause and cheers. Some of the soldiers had no one waiting there for them, which broke my heart. When I saw Travis all I could do was hug him and cry. The ordeal was over. I didn't want to let him go. He had lost weight but looked good. I was introduced to his battle buddies. They didn't have anyone waiting for them. So I grabbed each one of them and hugged them and cried some more. I thanked his sergeant for watching out for him and bringing him home. We got to stay with them until midnight then they went back to the barracks. It was still hard walking away, but the next day we could pick them up to spend the weekend together at a hotel and we took his battle buddies with us. My sister and her husband came down for the weekend, too. These soldiers ate everything they could get their hands on, watched TV, and went shopping. It didn't matter what we did, that was fine with us because we could reach out and give them a hug and kiss any time we wanted to. It is so hard to put into words the feeling of having the child you have raised go through something that you have no control over. And now he was home safe.

Katie Laude (wife):

The initial landing and the family time at Fort McCoy before coming home was very difficult for me. I had built up his return for months and months and pictured a movie-like reunion. This was not the case. When he got off the plane and came over to greet us he hugged and kissed all of the kids and then just quickly hugged me and moved on. He was still very much in military mode. As we were walking to the building where they were going to do a ceremony, he walked ahead of us talking to some of his men. I saw other couples walking arm and arm and staring into each other's eyes with tears across their faces. Not so with my husband. It was not the reunion I pictured. I later told him how hurt I was by all of this and he said he didn't even realize that was how he was acting.

Ben Peterson (child):

I kept having this dream that my dad and sister were with me waiting at the homecoming. All these people were around us. All the other soldiers got off the bus and all the other families were hugging. Then it was just us. We waited and waited and no one else came off the bus. In my dream, I thought my mom had died and they forgot to tell us. I'm so glad that dream didn't come true! When my mom really did come home, she looked kind of funny and didn't smell like Mom at first. Then we brought her home and she showered and put on her sweats and she hugged me a thousand times. Then she seemed like my mom again.

Stacy Westbrook (wife):

The best moment was the first time I saw him at the homecoming. I was sitting in the bleachers and the guys were all lined up in the gym. I scanned across all these guys that looked alike and then I saw his face.

Dorothy Trumble (mom):

I can't tell you what it was like for my daughter when she landed on US soil. We had decided that we would not go to her at her base, rather she would come home to us after her check-in. She didn't want us to pick her up at our airport; it was too public, she said. So that Saturday afternoon in May she rode up in a taxi. I stood at the front door with my other daughter and watched Alison walk up the front steps. I couldn't move. We all three of us stood there on the porch crying and laughing. I felt her hair and touched her cheek, just to check and make sure she was real. You have no idea what the feeling is. To have worried for so long and then to have your child standing in front of you, safe. I had to keep touching her and hugging her. All evening, I would walk by and give her a hug or a pat. She would squeeze my hand. The next morning was Mother's Day. I went to church with my two girls at my side and the biggest smile. I told everyone I saw that morning "My daughter Alison is home from the Air Force!" It was the absolute best Mother's Day I can remember.

Reflecting on Your Experience

As you plan for the day you will be together again, you may experience a range of thoughts, concerns, and emotions.

Lana Schmidtke (wife):

I have to say that in the 411 days that Dan was away from home, there were many, many times I thought about the changes all four of us were making. As the deployment wore on, we got used to our new life without him and, although I looked forward to the day he would again walk back into our lives, I also dreaded that day as it grew closer.

We had made a lot of changes in our lives, from downsizing the farm, to changing our looks with different hair styles and even colors, and also had done some major

changes in the house while he was away to help pass the time.
I had grown closer to the girls, more independent, and also
more sure of myself than I had ever been with Dan by my
side. After all, when he was here sharing every day with me I
often leaned on him for sharing the workload of raising the
kids and making daily decisions. Now after facing each day
on my own, being both mom and dad to the kids, mechanic
with the vehicles, and the main decision maker, I would soon
have to share those jobs again. Dan had left a quiet little
wallflower but was coming home to a very outgoing wife who
now was not afraid to take chances and let her voice be
heard.

The days leading up to Dan's coming home were days of
very mixed emotions. I wanted my best friend and husband
back in my life but I also wondered what having him home
would mean. How much had he changed and would he be
able to fit into the mix again? The girls had grown up so
much while he was gone. Would he accept their changes or
expect the little girls who wanted him to make the decisions
for them? Where Dan and I had always decided together
what we felt was best for them, I had learned to let them
make those choices for themselves. They were moving
beyond their teens into young adulthood.

That last month, when people would stop me and say
something about him coming home I would act very excited,
but on the inside I was scared to death.

I worried about who he would be. What changes had he
gone through? What had he seen, done, and felt during his
time living in a war zone? Would he be able to live with a
happy heart or had he experienced things that would change
his happy-go-lucky disposition to one of anger or fear?
Would he be able to accept the changes not only here at
home but also the changes that had been made in our
community, at his work place, and also here in the good ol'
USA?

I was scared to welcome him back home not knowing if he would feel like he belonged or even if we would fit together again. He had been the missing link in our family for so long, yet as the days wore on we had learned how to live without that missing link by filling in that space on our own.

I also worried about what our personal relationship would be like. Would the physical attraction still be there? What would it feel like to hold him and be held in return again? Would that big queen size bed I had been sleeping in on my own be big enough for the two of us again? A very small cot was his bed for over a year. Would he be able to adjust to the big bed and also to the feeling of having someone right there beside him again?

My biggest fear was what would I see when I looked at him? When I looked into his eyes would I again see trust and faith or uncertainty and hurt because of what he had seen and done?

Take a moment to reflect on the changes you have each experienced during this deployment. Some changes will be obvious, such as children growing older and taller, weight loss or gain, a redecorated house. Others may be less apparent at first.

Consider these questions:

- How has each person in our family changed physically? (physical appearance, weight, size and age—especially of children, health)
- How have our living environment and lifestyle choices changed? (where we live, type of housing, standard of living, proximity to family, house decor)
- Has my view of life changed? What is important to me now?
- How do I feel about professional choices we've made? (career choices, military lifestyle)

- What was my decision-making role before this deployment? During deployment? How do I expect it to change again? Do I feel more independent? Am I more self-confident? Has my childrearing and discipline philosophy or practice changed?
- Did this deployment affect us financially?
- What major events have taken place in our lives? Have we had a chance to work through those in a supportive way?
- Will friendships I developed in my service member's absence survive once we have each other to spend time with?
- Have I found new interests? How does my service member fit into these new activities? Will I give up something new when we're together or is there another solution?
- How has my service member changed? What kind of situations (e.g., seeing combat, famine; experiencing lack of privacy, regimentation) have changed his outlook? What changes have I noticed in our communications or during short leave periods?
- What are some other ways I have changed during the deployment? How has this changed my perspective? How could I use this experience to enrich my life and strengthen my family?
- Other than physical changes, how have our children or others around me changed during the deployment? Are there more changes I anticipate in the near future?
- Which of these changes have we talked about? If we haven't, why not and when do I think we should talk about them? Are they changes we can write about in letters or is talking in person more appropriate? Can I capture the changes in photos or journal entries?

- What are some of the things I miss about my loved one? What do I think my loved one misses about me? Do I think we still have those things to offer each other?
- In what ways has our relationship changed? Are we closer? Are there new concerns?
- What unplanned changes do I think might take place during our reunion?

There are many ways to reflect on changes. Read through your journal and letters from the deployment. Look through photos or scrapbooks at milestones (baby's first steps, holidays, etc.). Think about changes in your routine or friendships during the deployment. How will things be different when your loved one is home?

You might also look back at lists of projects and goals. Even if you didn't make all your goals (most people don't), you likely still accomplished a lot. What are some of those met goals? After looking at all you've learned, you might still feel a sense of having failed to meet some personal goals such as weight loss or saving money. Note those feelings and consider this time as your chance to meet those goals *with* your service member.

Whether the changes in your life are big or small, and no matter how well you've communicated with your service member, you may feel uncertainty about how those changes will be accepted. Going through this reflective exercise can help you anticipate which changes may be important to address early on in your reunion. Some may require simple introductions or updates while others may need more discussion, understanding, and time to work through.

Getting Ready for the Big Day

Heather Greene Hinckley (wife):

Six weeks before the homecoming I went into nesting mode, cleaning the house and office and kids. We live a disciplined life when Howard is here. He likes all the shoes in order: Dress Right Dress with the shoelaces in.

June Mickleby (mom):

I baked for days and days, all my son's favorite foods and desserts. I baked enough for all the single guys he was coming home with.

Jason Young (sailor):

We had some briefings on the ship over the two-week cruise home. They talked to us about our wives being more independent, how to politely say what we like about changes to the house or her hair (laughs). They said not to spend all our money in one place. And to go slow with things like, you know, sex. I called my wife at our last port and we decided to go away for the first weekend, just the two of us. I wasn't sure what to expect, really. I just wanted to be with her.

In the days leading up to homecoming, you may feel both excitement and uncertainty. You might keep busy getting ready for the homecoming event, making signs, buying favorite foods, talking with your service member about what you each hope for, and deciding who will come with you to greet your service member. Families who've been through more than one homecoming offer plenty of tips for getting ready for your big day:

- Talk before the homecoming about what you each want the day to be like.
- Don't plan anything elaborate for the first two weeks. (If you both want a big party or trip, have someone else do the planning and arranging so you don't add stress to your schedule and emotions.)
- Share as much detail as possible with each other about dates, times, and arrangements for the homecoming (e.g., large group gathering in gym or hangar, small group arriving by plane or bus, late night arrival,

mandatory briefings upon arrival) and find out how to get last-minute updates. Be flexible. Arrival times and sometimes arrival days change. Keep in contact with your key volunteer, ombudsman, or FRG leader. Update children, parents, and friends.

- Include children and parents in the planning and preparations. Expect children to be excited and possibly act out because they don't know how to channel their energy and feelings.

- Plan the pick-up. Will you meet somewhere or will your loved one be dropped off? If there is a homecoming event, decide together who will come to it. What will you do to keep busy in case of delay? Will you come straight home? What condition will your service member be in? (Perhaps in need of a shower immediately!)

- Plan activities for young children to keep them occupied leading up to and at the homecoming event.

- Find out what official duties you each will have, such as briefings, weapons checks, health evaluations, or work schedules.

- Talk about how you want to spend the first few days.

- Arrange for official military leave.

- Be flexible and have a backup plan because it may not turn out at all like you expect. The important thing is that you're together. You can figure it out as a family from here.

Who Should Be There?

One aspect of planning the day that causes stress for many families is deciding who should be at the homecoming and be part of the initial reunion time.

When Stacey Menocal was awaiting her husband's first Navy homecoming, her father, who spent twenty-three years in the Navy, gave her support group this advice: "Often, the rest of the family (your or his parents or siblings) will want to welcome him home. Discourage this. Tell them politely but firmly that you've earned a few days alone with your loved one. If they don't understand, too bad. They'll get over it."

Many counselors agree that for married couples, the first moments of reunion should be for them. It sends a message of commitment to each other confirming your life-long vows and gives children a feeling of stability and love among the chaos. Counselors tell service members to hug their spouse and then each child; it signals a good relationship between the parents and makes children feel comfortable.

If it's practical, include your children at the homecoming event. They are just as excited and nervous as you are, and being there gives them a tangible event to look forward to, plan for, and remember. It is a concrete beginning of change.

For parents of single service members, many factors weigh in on the decision. Heather Jacobsen shares, "We had to consider the cost for my husband and me to fly to our son's base and stay at a hotel. And then the rest of the family and hometown friends wouldn't get to be part of it. Or, we fly him home to see everyone. That worked better for us. Plus, he has time with his buddies to get settled first." But Gary Peters says, "there was no way my son was going to come home from war and not have someone there waiting. I went to get him."

When Regina Young's married son came home, she knew she would see him in person after he and his wife were settled. "It was enough for me to know he was home and safe. I did expect a phone call right away though! My daughter-in-law had told me she would hand him the phone if needed. I respect they needed time to reconnect before bringing in the whole family. I would want that, too," Regina says.

Talk about it with your service member so you work out a homecoming that meets everyone's needs.

Reunion Briefings

As you prepare for homecoming and reunion, you may have
the opportunity to participate in a military-sponsored reunion
briefing. Michelle Long says her reunion briefing was a four-hour
session that covered "everything from finance to medical benefits
to what to expect during reunification."

"Go if you can," says Bridgett O'Malley. "The briefing won't
tell you everything you need to know, but it will give you a whole
lot to think about and be aware of that you may not have taken
time to consider before."

In North Dakota, the state chaplain delivers the National
Guard briefing, a set of slides covering "the very basics," says
Lana Schmidtke. As a member of the State Advisory Council,
helping the military understand what military families need, Lana
acknowledges that it's hard to cover the topic of reunion in more
depth when no two situations are the same.

The biggest challenge, Lana and many other spouses agree, is
the timing of when you receive and use the information. You need
to be aware in order to prepare for homecoming. But you really
need the information the most in the months after your service
member is home and you are going through the reunion. Lana's
idea? Mentors. "Hearing in a briefing that these are things I will
be experiencing is great, but being able to talk one-on-one to someone who has been there, done that, or is going through the same
thing is the true helper," she says. "Reunion is hard and a very
long process. Many people do not want to share that they are having problems during this time. Their friends and family think they
should be happy and move on with life. Everyone should have a
mentor they can talk to about it."

In Vermont, Kara Kitchen-Glodgett's unit added a similar idea
to the traditional reunion briefing. "We brought in couples to speak
who had gone through it before. It was great. There is nothing like
asking someone who's been there; they know what your life is
really like."

The advice from these families is to attend whatever reunion programs are offered to prepare you for this journey. Read the information sent to you. Consider what applies. Find someone in a similar situation who is willing to talk with you several months from now. And don't be afraid to ask questions. "Chances are pretty good," says Bridgett, "that you are not alone. Someone has walked that path before."

What to Expect in the First Days

Each person touched by the deployment may have a different set of thoughts and worries during the first days of reunion.

First of all, it's been a long trip. Depending on the actual physical journey, the service member may have jet lag or a few days of simply adjusting to a new time zone and schedule. You'll all be tired. Tired from added responsibilities at home. From the worry during deployment and the stress of being apart. Children will be tired from feeling too grown up. Emotions tire everyone.

You'll all have mixed feelings. Your service member may feel good to be home and at the same time may feel hesitant about leaving the mission. You'll be excited to be together again but perhaps apprehensive about adjustments to the changes that have taken place. You just reflected on some of those changes. Independence. Self-reliance. Maturity. New interests. Physical changes. Home environment. Relationships. Everyone in your family has changed.

Everyone needs reassurance that they are loved, wanted, and needed. Everyone in the family wants to feel like their contributions are worthwhile. Each person in the extended family wants you to know they cared and worried, too.

For couples with children, your parenting and decision-making relationship will be strained. The family wants the service member to get involved again but not take over. Children need time to adjust to a parent who hasn't been around. Parents need time to adjust to making decisions together.

Couples need to court again. One or both of you will want romance and pampering. Strains from the deployment may cloud or confuse your feelings for each other.

Communicate your concerns, expectations, and feelings about homecoming. The more you communicate with each person in your family, the fewer misunderstandings or disappointments.

Things You May Be Thinking

Everyone in the family has a different perspective about the deployment and likely has different expectations for reuniting as a family.

How strong is our relationship? You may have become closer during this deployment. Or you may wonder if your friendship is strong enough to weather the changes and adjustments you know will come with reunion. If your relationship was troubled before the deployment or if you've had a hard time communicating, you're probably wondering how you'll make that bond stronger this time. Previous problems most likely did not go away during your separation. Commit to working at your relationship. Pick the aspect most important to you and write it down. Remind yourself every day to work on that part of the relationship.

What will our physical relationship be like? It's normal to feel excited and also a little anxious about resuming sexual relations. Take your time. You may find that everything falls into place. Or you may find that after spending several months or more apart, intimacy does not come easily. Rebuild your relationship and let the physical aspects come naturally.

Have I made good decisions? Making decisions during a deployment can be stressful. The decisions you made were the best under your own circumstances. Don't second-guess yourself. If you have confidence you did the right thing, so will those around you.

How has my loved one changed? You may be wondering: What did my loved one experience? Will his personality be the same? What will my role be in his life going forward? As a parent, you've tried to think of your deployed child as an adult. Deanna Wellsted, like many parents of young, single service members, came to a tough realization. "Your child is not going to come home a child. They are trained not to be. You need to accept that. Their focus won't likely be on family. They want to hang out with their friends," she says.

What is my service member thinking about? Your service member also wants the first moments to be right, wonders how you've changed, hopes your relationship will be strong, prays his children will be happy to have him home again, and fantasizes about making love to his partner. He also:

- wonders what you meant in some of your letters
- hopes you are aware of how demanding his schedule has been
- worries that young children won't recognize him or that teens won't need him anymore; wonders how well they dealt with the separation and what they think of him for leaving them; hopes they'll still think he's cool even though he doesn't know the latest phrases and hasn't seen the new hit movies
- has tried to convince himself that just because you coped well without him doesn't mean you want to be without him
- knows it will be hard not to feel like a stranger in his own home
- wants to understand and accept the decisions you made during the deployment
- feels guilty for missing important milestones such as the birth of a child, an anniversary, or special day
- wonders what cultural things he's missed; starts remembering how things work in America
- thinks about finances (especially if there have been major changes in the family such as a newborn or a change in spouse employment)

How will our children react? Children react differently to the homecoming and reunion depending on their age, their relationship with the deployed parent, and how you react and prepare. In general, children:

- hope the deployed parent will be glad to see them
- wonder if the parent will be mad about a report card or will yell at them for not completing a chore like they were supposed to
- may feel like the deployment had something to do with their behavior or that the parent *wanted* to be away from them
- feel resentful or angry with the parent for leaving
- feel anxious about how long the parent will stay home; may be worried about the parent leaving again soon
- wonder if the rules and lifestyle at home will change
- may worry about their parents' relationship if they sensed a troubled or abusive relationship before the deployment

Children may just be really, really excited, too—for themselves and for you. Once when my husband, Bob, returned home, our son, who was two, was so excited he tried to tell him everything all at once. Our son giggled as gibberish came out—he couldn't decide what words to put together first. Then he put his hand on our two faces and said, "Daddy you kiss Mommy!" He beamed with a big, big smile when we kissed!

Some of the things that impact how children respond include:

- how close the child was to the parent before the deployment
- how well the child understood the separation
- how the child reacted to events during the deployment
- how much and how well the child communicated with the deployed parent

What your child may be thinking:

- Will my dad (mom) be glad to see me?
- Will he be mad about my report card (or anything else that didn't go well)?
- How long will he be home? Will he leave again?
- What's going to change? What will it be like to have both parents in the house again? Do they still love each other?
- I'm so excited I can't think about anything else (and so I'm acting weird and don't know what to do with myself)!

Common Reactions and Preparation of Children and Teens

Infants (birth to one year old), toddlers (one to three years old)

It's hard for younger children to cultivate a relationship with an absent parent because so much of their understanding is based on physical senses. Their concept of time is very different from adults'. They won't really understand why the parent left them. It's also hard for young children to maintain any real communication with the parent. You can help your children by using pictures, audio recordings, and videos to keep a daily "presence" of the deployed parent. But even with the best of communication and relationship-building plans, children will react in ways you and your spouse should be prepared for.

To any child less than about eighteen months old, the returning parent will be a stranger. Your child will also be a stranger to the returning parent. A six- or twelve- or eighteen-month deployment is a big part of an infant or toddler's life. What does "daddy" mean to a child too young to have met this person or remember a past meeting? Perhaps it means a friend's dad, the picture she kisses goodnight, a voice on a recorder. Think of how your child reacts to strangers; it may be the reaction the deployed parent gets at homecoming.

Infants and toddlers may

- not know or remember the parent
- act shy, clingy, have a temper
- revert back to behavior they've outgrown
- be jealous

To help them get ready for the transition

> give them tangible reminders of the parent
> help them understand the parent's role in your home

Put the picture and voice together a few days before home-coming and explain to your child that this person will be living at home with you just like [insert the name of a father/mother figure similar to your spouse who lives at home with their child to help your child understand the relationship]. Remind your child for the next few days. Take your child around the house and answer questions like *Where will Daddy sleep?*

Infants may cry, fuss, or pull away from the returning parent and cling to the parent or caregiver they know. If they haven't been around deep, male voices, they may be frightened by a "new" male adult.

Unfortunately, many dads are deployed during the birth of their child or for much of a baby's first year. Childbirth and caring for infants is a profound and special time for all parents. It's especially hard to be separated at this time. Along with all the joy is the reality of caring for an infant. For the parent at home during deployment, it can mean exhausting days, disrupted nights, and feelings of being very alone as you struggle to meet your needs along with your baby's. It's also difficult for the deployed parent. First-time fathers may be anxious about their new role and the challenges that lie ahead. Those who've been there for the birth of other children may reminisce and regret not being there (or, be very happy they're missing those first few months!).

Service members returning to infants may find it useful to read about childbirth and infant care. (A good Web site for this is www.babycenter.com.) Learn about the development of children at different ages. You'll have a better understanding of what your spouse is going through, be more aware of what to expect, and have more confidence as an informed parent.

Realize that your child may not recognize you when you first return home because you haven't been a physical presence in his life during the deployment. Although pictures and voice recordings help, they aren't the same as a living person; young children need the whole package.

Go slow. Watch for the child's comfort zone. If a baby cries or a toddler pulls away when you approach, don't force contact. Stand as close as possible and let the child look at you, smell you, or reach out and touch you. Talk softly and often so an infant gets used to hearing your voice. To talk to toddlers, get down on the floor at their level.

Play. If you can get your child to laugh at you, you'll make a friend sooner. Be fun.

Stay close while your spouse feeds, dresses, or plays with the baby, changes a diaper, or gives the child a bath. Your child will probably watch you closely the first few times to make sure you don't touch or come too close. After a while, she will get used to having you there and you can take over with your spouse nearby. Eventually, your child will feel comfortable with you by yourself.

If you have other children, spend extra time with them. They may be feeling left out because of the baby, too.

Work on your relationship with your spouse. As a couple, you have many non-baby things to work out during your reunion. Children of any age are more comfortable with a parent when they know their parents' relationship is strong. Any effort you put into your marriage will pay off for the whole family.

Toddlers may act shy and clingy or display a temper. They may not fully recognize the returning parent. They may return to behaviors they've outgrown such as asking to be fed at meals even though they've been using utensils and feeding themselves for a few months, or wetting their pants even if they've been potty trained.

Infants and toddlers both may be extremely jealous of the time you spend with your spouse. To help them ease into the relationship, spend some time hugging your spouse while holding your child and encouraging your child to join in the family hug.

Preschoolers may
- feel like they caused the parent to go away
- act out for attention, test limits, react to too many changes
- revert back to behavior they've outgrown
- poke or hit to make sure the parent is real

To help them get ready for the transition
> give them tangible reminders of the parent
> help them understand the routine, what will change, and what will stay the same
> involve them in preparations

Preschoolers (three to five years old)

Preschoolers may feel guilty for "making" their parent go away. When a parent first returns, preschoolers may act out to get attention and to test limits with the new parent. They may demonstrate intense anger with too many changes and seem very demanding. They need time to get comfortable with the parent again and may even poke or hit the parent to test the realness of his presence. Once they get to know the returning parent again, they may seek extra attention and cling to the parent for fear he'll go away again. Use defined reassurances such as "I have to go to work now, but *I'll see you at dinner time.*"

Prepare preschoolers by explaining the reunion in concrete terms. Take them around the house and help them understand common routines that involve your spouse. Use specific examples of the way things used to be as well as how they may be when the parent returns. For example, "This is where Daddy used to sit for dinner. Should we set the same place for him when he comes home?" or "See the clothes Mommy left in her closet? Let's wash a couple of her favorite shirts so they smell fresh when she comes home." Again, explain that your spouse will sleep in your room with you, that he'll have to go to work during the day, and so on.

Children ages five to twelve may
- have mixed feelings they can't easily sort out or express
- resent a parent for missing out on things; try to hurt the parent (get back at him for being gone)
- be most excited, want to please, talk nonstop, ask lots of questions—be interested in every aspect

To get ready for the transition
> update your spouse on changes—children don't want to be seen as they were six to eighteen months ago
> help each child think of a few tangible things they can make for the parent and do together when the parent returns

---

Older children (five to twelve years old)

Older children are often the most confused about their emotions over a returning parent. A strong relationship and quality communication between the child and parent before and during the deployment is crucial. Children this age may resent a parent for missing certain events. If they feel hurt by the parent's absence, they may try to say or do things that would return some of that hurt to the parent. For example, a child might point out how the other parent handled things differently—or better.

At the same time, this age group is the most likely to run out to greet a returning parent. They want to please this parent and may feel guilty that they didn't do enough or weren't good enough while the parent was away. They might worry that the parent will discipline them for things that happened during the deployment. When given a chance, they'll also boast to friends about their parent's accomplishments and homecoming. You can expect these children to talk endlessly to update their parent on every detail of their lives during the deployment.

Prepare the returning parent by communicating beforehand the big and little ways in which your children have changed (clothes they wear, language, concerns, school activities, etc.).

Teenagers may

- exaggerate their individuality, exert their independence
- be concerned about freedom, rule changes
- be excited about the return and want closeness and private time with the parent

To help them get ready for the transition

> give them plenty of advance notice—fit into their schedule
> keep them involved with peers and other outlets
> encourage creative preparations

Teens (thirteen to eighteen years old)

They are moody. Irresponsible one minute, angels the next. Their hair and wardrobes change more frequently than the seasons. They want independence yet desperately need guidance. None of that will change just because a parent comes home.

Teens, in their careful attempt to gain independence from parents, may be unwilling to change their own plans to meet a returning parent at the homecoming site. Give them plenty of advance notice of the scheduled homecoming time frame (even if it's a week-long window) and simply say they don't have to come but it would mean a lot to the family if they did. Happily make arrangements to celebrate as a family later if something comes up at the last minute for your teen. With any luck, your willingness to make the choice theirs will prompt them into choosing family over friends.

As much as they're trying to be adults, teens are much like children when it comes to their emotions at homecoming time. They'll probably be concerned about rules and responsibilities, especially if your parenting style changed during the deployment. At the same time, they'll be really excited about the return if their relationship with the deployed parent is a strong one.

A New Beginning

For everyone in the family, homecoming marks an end to the long separation and the beginning of life together again. It may take several weeks for initial adjustments to iron out. Your family is adjusting to having your service member back in their lives. Your service member is adjusting to a more complex lifestyle that involves family intimacy. There may be experiences from the deployment that one or all of you need to reflect on and process. Your reunion may take extra time if the deployment was long or dangerous, if the deployment created serious financial issues for the family, if communication was more difficult than expected, if this was one in a series of deployments, if one of you was unfaithful to your relationship, or if anyone experienced a significant event such as an injury or death.

But don't worry about that just yet. In this chapter, you're making signs and buying food, getting ready for the big hug, the great day, the magic moment when, however brief it may be, the world seems right again.

Elizabeth Snow (wife):

I thought I was going to pee my pants I had been waiting so long. But I had the best view and didn't want to give up my spot. I could see him coming in the crowd. The uniforms all look the same, you know. The haircuts, too. Jarheads. These fighting men, brave men, good looking men coming home to us. They walked tall and proud, scanning the crowd, those grins coming across their faces as they recognized their loved ones. And then our eyes met. And I laughed. I cried. I waved. I wrapped my arms around his neck. He held me close at the waist. The world was loud around us. But all I could hear was his whisper in my ear. "It's so good to be home. I missed you so much it hurt. I love you, babe. I love you."

Chapter Two

Learning to Dance Again

There is a rhythm, a set of steps to a good dance. When you've been dancing solo, it takes a bit of practice and focus to dance with a partner, to make it work without stepping on the other's feet, to be able to adapt to different songs, and to find joy rather than work in the movements. Reunion also requires remembering moves, adjusting to new music, learning new cues, and trying not to step on each other's feet. You have to get used to a new environment, incorporate a loved one back into routines, relearn in-person communication, and process what has just happened in your lives. It is a bit like learning to dance again.

Ken Haugen (soldier):
    I felt like a guest in my own house.

Abby Sobaski (wife):
    I was so nervous. What if he changed? What if he doesn't like me anymore? But once we were back together, it was like he was gone for a minute. Then just getting used to each other was a challenge at first. I'm independent. I have a schedule—work out, eat at six. He wanted to eat earlier. He's messy. I'm clean and neat. It was all disrupted. But I realized some of it is true for anyone who is apart and then together. If I go visit my mom after not seeing her for a while, we have a little trouble. You have to remember and just get used to physically being in the same space again.

Heather Greene Hinckley (wife):

When he came home, it was like heaven for about two to three weeks, and then it was like the largest black cloud known to man came floating over our heads. I hated him and wanted him to leave again. He was angry with me because he didn't have the same role as when he left. This lasted for about two weeks. Thank God we have the relationship that we do and we were able to weave together, work together, and talk together to get through. Marriage is not a one-way street.

Deanna Wellstead (mom):

When my son came home on R&R, there was no structure to his day. He didn't know what to do with himself. As an SPC, he was told every day what to do over there.

Lana Schmidtke (wife):

Having Dan back that first month was one of the most trying times of my life. He sometimes felt overwhelmed with all the things the girls and I wanted to share with him. He lived with many other soldiers in a tent while he was gone and never really had time to just relax or be himself...then he came home and here are the three females in his life trying to spend every possible moment with him when he just wanted to be alone to take in his new surroundings and have some peace and quiet for once. Patience became our biggest challenge. We wanted to include him in everything, but he wanted his own space.

Susan Gillson (wife):

When Glen wasn't around, people made judgments without knowing our family situation. They didn't ask, they just assumed. People thought I was a single mom with four kids. Being able to show up with your spouse and show people you are "normal" too is a feeling that's hard to describe. Some people didn't know I had a husband. Some thought maybe he was just never involved in family stuff.

Some wondered who this new guy was. Very judgmental and it felt good to just quiet that by showing up with my husband.

Having Glen back home after seven years of being apart was "interesting" (laughs). It has been a total adjustment for all of us. He doesn't feel part of the routine. I try to help him feel welcome and valuable. It's hard because I've lived without a spouse for seven years. It's my house. I run it how I see fit. I'm so used to deciding things on my own, I have to remind myself to back off and let him be involved.

Jean Denney (fiancée):

When Reece came home after thirteen months, we did a home project together making bunk beds for the kids. He was frustrated because he couldn't find things—they weren't where they had been before he left.

Shannon Roberts (wife):

My husband came home a couple months earlier than the rest of the unit. He had a hard time with that because he felt he was deserting them. Since his flight was getting in at 11 p.m., I took his truck and parked it at the airport and he was going to drive home. There wasn't a big deal at the airport or anything since he was the only one at that time. We had big signs in the front yard welcoming him home and messages on the convenience store signs in the town next to us. (Our town has about 500 people.) We couldn't possibly go to bed, so we waited impatiently for his arrival. He walked in the house and the dog barked at him not knowing who he was until he spoke. We all just ran and hugged him. The kids were just a nervous wreck waiting. It was like the anticipation at Christmas when you were little! They adjusted quickly and much better than I anticipated. I had explained things to them ahead of time. We had lots of hand outs that we read telling us what to expect. He kind of just wandered around the house, checking things out...seeing what changed or stayed the same. He has his favorite old hunting dog that he had to go greet also. The next few days he spent adjusting to climate and sleep.

He only took a couple weeks off before returning to civilian work. Looking back on that now, he wishes he would have taken longer. He doesn't think that was enough to fully adjust. Looking back, I feel it was all worth it. There are so many ups and downs along the way. You learn from each experience and everyone grows from it as a person. It makes you look at things in life in a whole new way. It teaches you to pick what you stress over, to live each day as if it were the last, and it definitely teaches you strength and faith. He—and we —are so proud of what he has done.

Julie LaBelle (mom):

(Just before her son came home): Initially, I had visions of a warm, fuzzy reunion filled with movies and family meals and lots and lots of talking. Because we have a good relation-ship and he's always been such an open, easy-going kid I also expected that he would share all of what he has seen and done while in Iraq.

I have already been told by two other mothers to lower my expectations. They told me to expect to not see him much, that he'll be distant and not talk about war itself, but only interactions he's had with other Marines. My husband, Ed, a retired Marine, has also warned me that since Alex is coming from such a male dominated world under rough circumstances, that his social graces may be entirely lacking and that his language will be anything but PG-rated. I also feel that I need to leave behind the "mothering" part of me. This experience has definitely shifted him from a young person I can nurture into a man. My role will change now, and I'm not quite sure what it will be.

I definitely see the wisdom in keeping the guys with their unit for a while, rather than letting them come right home. I think they've been out drinking every night and there was a lot of catching up on romance, too. After the trying times these young men have been through together, it was good to be reintroduced to society along with the men they've just served with.

(Three weeks later): Alex has reached the end of his leave and goes home Thursday after three weeks with us. I was lucky. The first five days he talked about the war and answered all my questions. Then he said, "Now we're done with that, and we need to move on." Some chairs dropped over on the deck during a windstorm and the poor kid practically jumped out of his skin. After two weeks at home he crashed. He fell into a deep, deep sleep and woke only to eat and lie back down. This lasted two days. At one point he sat up and said, "I've got to beat somebody up" and passed back out. I was concerned, but after talking it over with Ed, we realized that after Alex returned to the States he had purchased a vehicle, found a new apartment, retrieved everything he owned from storage, reunited with family in California, and had gotten himself to Washington to meet scores of people. When everything was accomplished he collapsed. When he woke up again—voilà—he was the same old happy, cheerful kid he was before. Our reunion was wonderful!

Kara Kitchen Glodgett (wife):

Our reunion was like an out-of-body experience. The anticipation was horrible. Months before the homecoming, I went into nesting mode. I redecorated our bedroom, got things in order. I didn't sleep for a week before the homecoming. Some wives didn't eat, but I ate everything in sight. He came home very fit and I was eating Ben & Jerry's comfort food.

That first night I thought "Who are you?" I knew him, but it felt a little like an arranged marriage. Someone is sleeping in my bed. Weird. It was like a first date again—exciting.

We were all exhausted. Talking so much. Well, I did a lot of talking, anyway. He wasn't ready to share right away. My advice is to give him space and allow him to come into life again. Don't change kids' routines right away. I gave him a couple weeks to just observe and jump in when he wanted to, then asked for more help. For about three months, we had bumps, then less. It took us about a year to get back. Communication is key. I believe in saying "I need this."

Katherine Leland (wife):

Having my husband deployed just after our first anniversary was extremely challenging. We had just purchased and moved into our first home when Jacob was deployed for thirteen months. Once he was gone, "our" home turned into this empty place that later became "my" home, since he wasn't there. When he returned, it was and continues to be this enormous transition as we try to put the pieces back together. Sometimes I really resent the Army for taking Jacob away, but he came back and I am blessed that he did come back.

Lauren LaBelle (teen sister):

When my brother came home, I was so relieved that nothing had happened to him. I didn't know how the reunion would go. Like, would he be hostile? Would he want to be hugged and know he's home and enjoy this? What would I do? My mom had told me not to mess with him because he just got back from war. That made me chuckle, but knowing that this was true kind of set the boundaries. But that didn't stop us from reverting to our old ways of hitting and yelling. As bad as that may sound, it was nice to have that back and be able to do that again. I would never have guessed I would miss it quite as much as I did. Now that he is home in the States, I don't really think about the time when he went overseas. Nothing really has changed too much between us. We're still the same brother and sister we always have been, only we see each other a fraction of the time we used to. He still annoys me, and still can be a complete butthead, but I kind of think that the war has changed him. He doesn't talk to me as much as he used to, and his personality has kind of changed, but the way we act when we are around each other is still enjoyable.

Katie Laude (wife):

Our middle son, Sam (age seven) would not even look at Tom when he got off the plane. When he eventually warmed up to him, we had the problem that Sam literally would not let Tom out of his sight for months.

Sarina Hess (mom):

I had two sons stationed in Iraq. My eldest son owned his own mechanic shop and I was in charge of the accounting area of both his personal and business finances. My other son's affairs were taken care of by his father. It was a very difficult time for us at home since their safety was always an issue. Upon their return it was of course a great joy to see and just touch them, but was also difficult watching them pay special attention to ditches and even pop cans. Well trained, they were watching for explosive devices! I have to add, this was the toughest time of my life.

Different Worlds

The world your service member is leaving is likely very different from the world at home. He may have seen and participated in aspects of a mission many of us don't see in our nightmares: famine, filth, terrorism, intended death. Some of the things your loved one was part of he may not be comfortable with. Not only does he have that to sort through, but he may be worried about you or his children asking questions like "Daddy, did you hurt anyone?" Your service member may feel wounded, if not physically, then emotionally or spiritually.

**Top advice from military families
for the first weeks and months of reunion:**

- Take care of yourselves.
- Listen—openly communicate.
- Don't compare your situation to other people's.
- Be patient and flexible.
- Reassure each other, show you care with your words and actions.
- Trust each other.
- Couples: Court, reestablish intimacy.
- Expect children to test you, change routines slowly.
- Have a sense of humor.
- Don't argue about who had it worse. Recognize you each had your challenges and unique experiences.
- Give it time.

During this deployment, your service member may have faced a constant life-or-death stress. He likely was in an environment of giving and taking orders, needing to know whom to trust, dealing with the fact that there is an enemy, and having few outlets. Daily comforts may not have included things like a hot shower in clean water, soft toilet paper, privacy, and gentle intimacy.

Now, he must go from that environment where life and death depended on following orders and being on watch 24x7. And you want to discuss, maybe even negotiate, and make decisions together. This is a big adjustment, even if you both want the same thing.

He may feel torn between wanting to be home with his family here and wanting to be helping the service members he just left or who replaced him on this mission.

Even if your service member was on an assignment that took him to exotic ports of liberty, he had to sleep where he works. He was on someone else's roster and call.

During the first few days at home, there are physical adjustments to time zone differences, jet lag, and a completely new schedule. The intensity of the deployment (especially for those in humanitarian efforts or dangerous situations) is suddenly replaced with the routine of life at home. Their entire surroundings have changed, from a sleeping bag on the ground or a cramped bunk to a comfortable bed and quiet house at night, from taking orders to answering family questions. There is also the adjustment of getting back to an often chaotic American lifestyle. He may have trouble communicating, eating, sleeping, or being intimate.

As you go through the first weeks of reunion, keep in mind that much of what you will all be adjusting to has little to do with you and much to do with simply coming from different worlds, different experiences, and learning to dance together again.

Keith Browne (Marine):

I was living with dirt in my face all the time. I received and gave orders. It was 24x7 on guard. And now I'm supposed to mow the lawn and talk about what I want for dinner? Honestly, I spend a lot of time in the bathroom. Clean, hot water and privacy are my way of getting back into the home life!

Lori Zimney (mom):

Our son Billie was so immature, a very materialistic person before he deployed. He would tell you the brand and color shirt he wanted for Christmas. He is not as demanding now. It surprised us. Billie came home thinking people here take too many things for granted. They are so trivial. He had difficulty dealing with daily things because his perspective changed so much.

Michelle Long (wife):

David deployed for eighteen months. As a wife and mom I wear twenty thousand hats. I know what I need to do and how to fit it all in. Suddenly I'm thinking about what my husband wants for dinner and what he might want to do tonight. And he's dealing with what he's seen and done and had to live with. In Ramadi, they trucked in river water and were not able to open their mouths in the shower. When he got home, he just wanted a hot shower with clean water. There they scoured the roads looking for bombs. It's hard for the soldiers not to worry about items on the road here.

Intimacy

Dr. Jennifer Morse, retired US Navy captain and former chair of psychiatry at Naval Medical Center in San Diego, tells service members that even though they may have dreamed about how happy they'd be if they could just be back with family and friends, reconnecting with loved ones after deployment, especially a war deployment, isn't always easy. "Your identity and view of the world have grown and changed and they've been shaped by your experience in a combat and operational environment," she says. "It's natural that your relationship will be affected." One of the natural responses is that the service member "may resort to safer emotional ground such as arguing about finances, sex, disciplining kids, what you want to do with your life." It may be difficult or slow going reestablishing intimacy. And it may come in familiar or new ways.

Paula Church says that when her husband returned home, "We had no problems in the sex department. It was like a honeymoon! He was very sweet and romantic and wanted to make sure everything was okay." For Teresa Sanderling, however, it wasn't so easy. "Sex was the farthest thing from our minds," she says. "It was like I didn't even know this person. He was so distanced from me. After two months, we finally went to a marriage counselor." Rita

Kim shares, "Lee was very gentle and quiet. We held hands and really focused on our time together alone, sharing our thoughts and stories. We got to know each other again. Even though we wrote many letters, it is still strange to be together in person and say things to each other's eyes."

When working to reestablish intimacy with your partner, expect awkward moments, especially the first few times you are back together. You'll probably be operating at quite different speeds. Plan private time together without children, parents, friends, or relatives. Tune in to your partner. Talk, cuddle, be playful. Realize it's normal to feel strange together, especially after long separations. Be patient and gentle. Communicate your sexual desires, but remember that you don't need sex in order to be intimate. Hugs, kisses, caresses, and whispers express love, too. Build trust and comfort. Take precautions against pregnancy unless you've planned a pregnancy together.

Remember that fatigue is common during initial reunion. If your partner is too tired to be with you physically, it's not a sign of rejection. Sleep in each other's arms or use some other form of intimate touch to connect. Limit alcohol intake. Resolve issues of anger, resentment, distrust, jealously, or anxiety; they greatly reduce your ability to be intimate and loving. Have fun and enjoy being with one another.

Stacy Westbrook says she and her husband "put the kids to bed early. We sit on the swing and drink coffee. It's that simple sometimes."

Take fifteen minutes each day.

You will eventually fall into a daily living routine. How you structure that routine is important. Listen to each other and discover your current needs. While all the time you spend together is important, there are fifteen very important minutes each day that can set the groundwork for reconnecting and building your relationship.

Courting Ideas

- Say, "I'm glad I married you" or "I'm happy I'm in this relationship with you."
- Hold hands as you walk.
- Give your partner a back rub or a foot massage.
- Write a poem for each other.
- Hug your partner from behind; kiss the back of his/her neck.
- Ride bikes together. Watch the sunset. Build a snowman.
- Sit on the same side of a restaurant booth.
- Share a milkshake with two straws.
- Plant a tree together in honor of your relationship.
- Look into one another's eyes as you talk.
- Play board games.
- Take on a fun challenge together, such as hiking up a mountain or learning to surf.
- Say "I love you" every time you think it.

Five minutes in the morning

Some people like to receive a kiss first thing in the morning. Others like to sleep in and just get a kiss goodbye when a spouse leaves for work. Others like to eat breakfast together. What would your loved one like to do in the morning?

Five minutes after work

During the first five minutes after a long day at work, few people enjoy being grilled, criticized, given a list of problems, or hearing everyone's complaints about the day. Some people like to spend a few minutes by themselves, changing clothes and mentally making a transition from work life to home life. Others like to be greeted at the door (by a spouse, child, dog) and welcomed into their home. Some like to retreat to their own special place for a while; others need a few minutes of sharing. Who gets home first? What would you like? What would your loved one like? What happens after the time alone or the greeting? Most couples like to start the evening off with a positive conversation; some families use the dinner table to relate the day's events and connect with each other. Whatever time and environment you choose, make sure you give each other at least five minutes of your full attention.

Five minutes before bed

Every family has a different routine just before bed. Some couples go to bed at different times. Others make love before going to sleep. Some people like to read in bed while others like to go to sleep right away. Most people have a hygiene ritual; make sure yours doesn't infringe on your spouse's. The last few minutes before you go to sleep should be pleasant ones. A good feeling helps you sleep better and puts you in a better state of mind for tomorrow.

Counselors suggest that you work on reestablishing an intimate relationship with those closest to you before taking on the challenge of redistributing responsibilities and other household or family challenges. One of the steps to reestablishing intimacy is open communication.

New Kind of Communication

For many months now you have communicated by letter, phone, email, and care package. You had time to choose what you would share and not share. When you were done sharing, you went back to your separate life and had time before your next communication. Now that the deployment is over, how often do you see each other? What are all the messages you are trying to read at once. Now you see facial expressions, body language. You hear laughter or crying. You can choose to shop and sleep and eat together—or not. It's wonderful and also overwhelming.

Open communication is the number one thing military families I interviewed said is the key to any reunion. Katherine Leland says, "If I could give any advice to other couples, it would be to communicate as much as you can in any way possible. Without communication, the other person doesn't know what to do. Communicate in any form; crying, laughing, talking, sharing, taking walks, grocery shopping together, emails are all ways that couples can allow for growth and sustain a relationship." Never go to bed angry. If you deal with an issue or misunderstanding right away, there is less chance of building resentment or further misunderstanding.

"Sometimes there is so much communication, you go on overload," warns Paula Church. "Don't over analyze. Maybe he didn't mean anything by that look. Let it go. If you think it's something, then ask. Work it out every day. Keep little things little."

Learning to talk face-to-face again can be challenging for any family member. After months of writing messages, it may be awkward trying to find the right words in person and in that moment. If you were successful communicating by letter during the deployment, try writing a few letters when you're first together again. Read the letters while you're together as a way to start the conversation, especially if the subject at hand is a hard one to discuss. It won't be long before your letters become short notes or you're back to talking freely face-to-face.

Your service member may have had deployment experiences he doesn't know how to explain to you. He may have witnessed killing, wounding, and disfigurement of enemy soldiers, civilians, his own comrades, and close friends. He may have lived under a 24x7 threat of hard-to-find improvised explosive devices and guerilla warfare tactics. He may have seen firsthand the effects of severe poverty and famine. Female soldiers may have had an added strain of fighting to defend a culture that does not fully accept them in this role.

The deployment situation may also have been a tremendous strain on your family at home. The media provides graphic, up-to-the-minute updates, usually emphasizing tragedy and disaster, often giving the impression that it is happening everywhere in the deployment area. Rumors, misinformation, and speculation about the welfare of loved ones amidst all the news only serves to heighten family stress. You may have experienced additional stresses at home that the service member was not part of. Many of these challenges may be equally difficult to discuss.

Stacy Westbrook offers, "The best advice I have for a family is just to be there for that loved one; you have no clue what they have experienced."

New Routines

Some of the first real adjustments we notice during reunion are breaks in our routines. There is another person to incorporate into home life, someone whose routine has also changed over the months.

Jennifer Christy (wife):

Tom and I had been married five months when he was called to active duty with two weeks' notice. He deployed for seventeen months to Iraq. I was nervous about our reunion. The Army prepared me for the fact he had been in a war zone. He saw things he won't want to share. After a month at home, he was still quiet and still adjusting to civilian life. At the core, he's still the same person I fell in love with. The best moments have been just sitting next to him, touching him, looking into his eyes.

I had been thinking so much about him, I was surprised at how hard it was for me to adjust. The first Sunday he was home, I had to break my routine. I always read half the paper, ate breakfast, read the other half of the paper. I was so used to my routine, it was overwhelming and stressed me out that this other person was in it. I didn't expect that. I should be excited to spend time together. He let me have my alone time and then after a little while I called him back over to read the paper with me. That was the most challenging thing, just incorporating him into the little me times. We slowly readjusted.

Kathee Santiago (wife):

I am a retired Army first sergeant. I thought I could handle just about anything when it came to deployments. My husband, also retired from the Army after twenty-five years, decided to go to the Middle East as a contractor. He started in Kuwait and ended up in Afghanistan. He came home after five years of deployment. Talk about readjusting! Even all the little things are becoming big things: sleeping together, sharing the bathroom, cooking meals, disciplining the kids. I am very proud of my husband and my family for everything we have been through.

There may be some routines that you need to address right away in order to keep your family and household running, but try to overlook minor changes or annoyances in the first days so you can focus on your communication and being together again. Chores, schedules, and who gets the bathroom first in the morning can all be worked out over time. When you get to that point, here are a few tips for helping routines fall into place.

Talk about what is important to each of you in your routine. Teresa Sanderling told her husband, "I need to eat breakfast first thing or I'm grouchy and it takes me a while to wake up so I prefer to talk about anything serious later in the day."

Get out a calendar or daily planner and discuss obligations, work schedules, kids' routines and activities. Bring a returning parent up to date on bedtime rituals and other important elements of your family's routine.

Try not to change kids' routines right away. Kids feel safer and adults feel more comfortable, too, when you know what to expect. This helps ease everyone into other things that are new.

Post notices, schedules, house rules, and reminders on the fridge or other central location for all to see and remember. Be open to how your daily habits or activities may be affecting someone else. See it from another's view and be open to trying it their way for a couple weeks.

Rebuilding Relationships Through the Changes

Lana Schmidtke (wife):

You expect each person to change; we're taught to expect it. But then when you're together again, you think it will go back, that we'll be our old selves. Or maybe that we'll be able to adjust quickly to any changes. But really, it took us fifteen months to make these changes. What makes us think it won't take that long to get used to them or to make new changes together? Working together we are finding that new normal and although sometimes it gets frustrating knowing that life will never again be as carefree and easy as it was our first eighteen years together, we are building a new normal for our next eighteen years.

Remember those reflections from chapter one on the changes that have taken place during deployment? Now would be a good time to update the list! In the first few weeks or months of reunion, you are likely discovering many changes. Some are wonderful. Some may concern you. There may be small things such as your preferences in food, clothing, or recreation. Or bigger things such as financial issues or career changes. Or even more serious challenges such as an illness or injury.

There are a few things you can do early in your reunion to help build new relationships with your loved ones and begin the next phase of your life together.

Spend time alone with each family member.

Activities as a family can strengthen your overall family bond, but the time you spend listening and sharing individually is what builds trust and intimate connections. Give each person your full attention for at least fifteen minutes a day and try to do one activity you both enjoy together at least once a week.

Stay involved in children's activities and interests.

Let a returning parent know about upcoming schedules and which activities are most important to the children. Make room for your returning spouse to take on special roles with your children and to spend time alone with each child.

Address previous issues.

Separations don't usually solve problems. This may include serious issues such as substance abuse or violent tendencies. Commit to working on your relationship together and keeping your family safe and healthy.

Honor what your service member has been through and continue to support military colleagues.

Lana Schmidtke notes that people around you will not necessarily understand the need to support your service member's mission. "The media portrayed everything bad," she said. "Some people around us ask why we are still in Iraq. People who were there know why it's still important we are there."

Before Linda Bong's husband, Daryl, left for his fifteen-month deployment to Afghanistan, he put up a flag pole and she bought a flag. "When he came home, he flew the flag at half mast. It's his way of honoring those who are still there. He said the flag will go up again when they all come home."

Appreciate life.

Nancy Mulcahey says that during her sons' deployments, "We all got very close. We realized we had said we loved each other more than ever. Now when the boys see us or when they are leaving to go home there is always a kiss and hug. On the phone now we always say 'Love you. Bye.' It has made us realize the fragileness of life. Before the boys left in December, my husband and I had a bad motorcycle accident. That made us realize things can happen in a minute's time. Then my husband had a heart attack in January of this year, so we all just value our time together. I think the boys have adjusted fine back to their private lives. But I don't feel sloughed off to the background. My oldest is getting married on a cruise to Mexico this May so we are all planning a great time."

Let go of the past.

Some things that happened while you were apart, you can simply let go of. Lana Schmidtke had written two letters to her husband, Dan, on most days of the deployment. The first was to get things off her chest and the second, without her reactive emotions, she mailed to him. "Those letters I wrote to him pouring my heart out each day went into a shoe box that I intended to share with him when we could read them together. But that never happened. When he called me from Colorado to let me know he was back stateside I decided that those letters were no longer important so I took them outside and threw each one into the burning barrel. Those things were in the past and although during the deployment I thought I wanted him to someday read them and know what we went through, that was the past and we had nothing but the future to look forward to."

Stick to your budget.

Abby Sobaski says, "It's always about money, isn't it? He came back from his first deployment with a lot of money saved. He wanted to spend it on a big TV. I wanted to save it for our wedding and a house."

Your service member may not remember how much money your family needs. Perhaps your family's financial needs have changed during the deployment because of a new baby or a change in employment. Spending money you don't have will create more trouble later. Also, you may need to rethink your budget. The end of a deployment means changes in pay and allowances once again. At the same time, if you can afford it, Kara Kitchen-Glodgett suggests buying something special for your family. "It feels like you have something to show for it. Forest bought rugs in Afghanistan. They smelled like a camel, but he wanted something. When he came home, we bought a boat. We just said life is short and that's something we'll enjoy as a family." She adds, "Budget for it and make sure you know what changes you'll have to make in order to make it work financially."

Expect children to test limits.

Susan Gillson says her two oldest children, ages nine and eleven, "knew about living with Dad, but the two youngest, ages six and seven, never knew what it was like to have Dad in the house full time. If they don't get the response they want from Dad, they go to me because they are used to how I do things. I have to help them learn that Dad can have an opinion that's different from mine and we have to respect Dad's decisions too."

Discuss changes in discipline procedures when you're away from children and implement them over a period of weeks.

Recognize and address unhealthy adjustments.

Most couples and families adjust positively within a few weeks or months depending on the circumstances of the deployment and reunion. However, it's important to recognize signs that you are not getting back in sync or that you're doing so in a negative way. Danger signs include depression, social isolation, substance abuse, excessive anger, and violence. If you or your spouse think you may need help individually or as a couple, don't hesitate to ask for it. Understanding the source and addressing it promptly can help prevent issues from escalating.

When Is It Time to Seek Help?

"There are many things to look for," says Chaplain Randy Imhoff of Pastoral Counseling Center of Northern New York. "The best thing to do is schedule an appointment with a chaplain soon after reunion to get help discussing reunion/reintegration: your expectations, changes, adjustments, intimacy, children, finances, and so on. Also look for any significant changes in the relationship: distance of one or both partners, increased arguing, arguing over what used to be insignificant issues, or any indication of PTSD. Some of these things will get better with time. However, if things to do not get better, seek help right away, do not wait.

"Just about every circumstance could be handled better by getting help sooner. Most people wait too long from the onset of a problem before seeking help. When they do seek help, they want the quick fix for a problem that is ingrained in the relationship.

"Specifically, the biggest issue for people coming to see a chaplain, especially couples, is communication. Seeking help early when communication problems arise is better than waiting until there is emotional disconnection, strong contempt toward the other spouse, and built up resentment.

"In my years as a chaplain, I can count on one hand the number of people who have come to see me before a problem really became a problem. Most wait until the relationship has eroded to the point where one or both are thinking separation or divorce before seeking help."

Happy Reunions

As you learn to dance again, keep in mind these tips for a happy reunion:

- Communicate openly and honestly.
- Accept each other and the changes that have taken place. Express pride in each other's accomplishments. Appreciate and encourage further growth.
- Make changes slowly. Don't be too quick to take over or give up a responsibility. Take time to understand how your family or the circumstances have changed since you were last together. If you need to change children's routines or discipline rules, do so gradually.
- Take care of yourself. Eat healthy foods, get sleep, exercise.
- Limit criticism. When needed, keep it constructive. To resolve conflicts, stay on the subject. Don't accuse, blame, confront, or bring up the past.
- Reaffirm your love and commitment. Jealousy is often caused by insecurity.
- Take your time relating deployment stories. Get to know your family again and work the stories in gradually.

- Stick to a budget. It doesn't have to be expensive to be fun or romantic.

- Be patient and flexible. People may look or act differently, but they are the same people you know and love.

- If you think anyone in your family would benefit from talking with a chaplain, doctor, or other professional, do not hesitate to seek that guidance. Everyone wants each of you to be healthy and happy.

Chapter Three

Stress and Other Things
We Worry About

There are many responses to the stresses of deployment and reunion. Sometimes working through this stress is a matter of talking it out with the right person. Sometimes it requires the guidance of a professional. Keep in mind that stress can affect everyone in your family, including children. This chapter is meant to give you an idea of what some families experience and to be a starting point for you if someone in your family shows symptoms or behavior that concerns you.

Anatonya Jackson (wife):

Robert and I have never had secrets. We've always shared everything with each other. We're very close. It's just the two of us, no kids. We wrote each other every day during his deployment. I just knew in my heart we would be okay when he came home.

In the reunion briefing, they told us that our guys might need someone else to talk to because of what their unit had gone through. So I prepared myself for that in my mind, although because of our closeness I thought Robert and I might be different.

The first three days of homecoming were perfect. The fairytale kiss, making love, hearing his laugh again, just being together. Around the fourth day, Robert called his dad and asked him to come stay with us. My father-in-law served in Vietnam. I understood this might be what Robert needed, but I wasn't really prepared to share him so soon. His dad arrived

the next day. They went on long walks, they sat in the back
yard and drank coffee together, things I wanted to be doing.

Robert was polite and respectful to me that week, but
seemed tired and not the romantic man who came home to
me just a few days before. I couldn't help feeling hurt that it
wasn't me he was talking to. The day before he left, my father-
in-law came over to me in the kitchen and put his arm
around my shoulder. He said, "Thank you, Tonnie, for being
there for my son. Your letters, your constant love brought him
through this deployment. He had a lot of things to worry
about and it made a big difference that he didn't have to
worry about you."

Well, all the tears I had been holding back all week just
came pouring out! I stood there hugging my father-in-law
and crying my eyes out. He cried, too, and said, "I know,
honey. Me, too." And then I understood why this week had to
happen. Robert needed both of us.

Robert calls his dad every Sunday. That's their time. And
during our time, he's every bit the man I love. I've learned it's
not about sharing all our secrets. It's about trusting each
other and loving each other even when there are things we
can't share. Our relationship is even stronger now and so is
his relationship with his dad.

Lana Schmidtke (wife):

Dan saw much pain and suffering along with the sights
and sounds of war in Iraq. A soldier was killed. Another
fought for his life and survived, with the loss of his arm.
Today, twenty months later, there are still occasional
reminders of what we could see so plainly when Dan first
returned home. Occasionally the girls or I will catch him just
gazing off into space and we know that he has traveled back
to Iraq. He is not so quick to jump when a loud noise goes off
like he first was and he has grown very trusting of people
again. I no longer have to fear accidentally touching him in

What Service Members Need to Adjust at Home

Dr. Mike Colson, a retired Navy commander, estimates that 45% to 50% of service members returning from assignments during the Global War on Terrorism need to talk about their experience. Between 15% and 18% need more than a conversation; they need a regular program with a counselor. He estimates 1% may have serious mental illness. He cautions that when we change as individuals, some of that change is negative and we may take it out on our families and loved ones, as well as our friends and community. If we delay getting help, the negative behaviors become ingrained. The good news, he adds, is that in change there is also an opportunity to seize our goals, hopes, and dreams.

According to Col. Bob Stewart, chief of the Department of Behavioral Health at Fort Belvoir, Virginia, several factors affect how well a service member adjusts when coming home:

- family support vs. lack of support
- unit support vs. lack of support, especially when the service member changes duty stations upon returning from a deployment
- financial stability vs. money problems
- availability of local treatment vs. limited or no treatment, as would occur for those far from a military or VA medical facility
- understanding within the community vs. working with other service members with no deployment experience or, especially for Guard or Reserve members, going back to a community that doesn't understand the prolonged effects of a deployment experience

the night because he no longer goes to bed "on guard" and has learned to trust me lying beside him.

Adam Mitchell (soldier):

There was a fog around me. I felt like I should be able to touch it but it was just out of reach. I didn't like crowds. I thought I was going crazy. My doctor had a good way of thinking of it.

He said I was "coming down from an adrenaline rush." Being on call 24x7, separated from family, high level of alert for a long time. I was crashing from the adrenaline. He said to give myself two weeks.

I had two weeks of transitional leave with my family to adjust and get back into family life. He was right. After two weeks, I felt like myself again.

Heather Greene Hinckley (wife):

I was driving on a four-lane road. A bicycle came out from a side street and Howard grabbed the steering wheel and nearly steered us into oncoming traffic. When I asked him what he was doing, he said he had seen the bicycle, with a bag on the side of it, and had forgotten that he wasn't still overseas.

Jolaine Barnes (wife):

Keefe had trouble feeling comfortable at social gatherings or even at a restaurant. We had to find a place to sit or stand that had a wall or solid structure behind him so he could always know that no one was coming up behind him.

Keefe Barnes (Marine):

You go from always being on watch, expecting someone to try to kill you, looking for anything unusual, and then you're supposed to be nice and give people the benefit of doubt. Letting down your guard can't happen overnight. I'm not sure I'll ever completely let it down.

Mark Sites (soldier):

You have no idea what stress is until you've been in combat. You live on the adrenaline rush. You're used to it all the time. Then when you come back, it's not there anymore and you have to find something to get back to how it was. I need to go sky diving or rock climbing or even street racing. It might sound strange, but doing these things makes me calm again.

Shannon Roberts (wife):

Josh had some issues with having a short fuse and coping with some situations in a proper manner. He immediately went to the doctor to discuss those and got on some medicine. That has helped a great deal. I think the most important thing people need to know about that is to not ignore signs of issues. Even the small ones should not be overlooked.

Deidra Washington (wife):

Louis came home very angry. He yelled at our son, Keenan, all the time for making a mess at the table or leaving his clothes lying around. His voice was always cross and impatient. I thought maybe he just needed time to get used to us again, to get used to living in a normal house. But it got worse before it got better. He started throwing things, first at the door or wall. Then one day he threw his boot at Keenan. I told him to get out. I said, "I love you but you have to get control of yourself before you come back into this house." He turned around and said he was sorry. But the next morning it was more of the same, this time directed at me. When he left for work, I called the chaplain and told him Louis needed help.

I did not know how to support Louis and I did not want him to hurt anyone. I was afraid if I waited or just made threats to kick him out, that one of us would be seriously hurt first. Louis was mad that I had called about him. But

now it has been a couple months that he has been in
counseling and he is doing much better. One day I know he
will realize that I made that call for all of us and because I
love him.

Getting Help

Sometimes when loved ones come home, we have a tough
time knowing if what they're going through is "normal" or whether
they're having more serious issues.

Many symptoms are the same for different conditions and
responses. For example, for someone experiencing anxiety or
anger, it may be a short-lived response to the adjustments of
reunion or it may be an indication of a more serious issue. A
professional can help identify what the issues are and the best
way to deal with them. On the following pages, you'll find some
common symptoms along with advice and ideas for where to
turn next.

Anger

What to look for:

- "short fuses" or outbursts of anger or violent behavior
- increasing impatience
- rough handling or abuse of loved ones
- threats to hurt someone
- a feeling of "walking on eggshells" so you don't make the
  person angry

What you can do if your loved one has outbursts of serious anger
or violence:

- Make sure you and other family members are safe; go to
  a neighbor's house or call 911 if necessary.
- Stay calm; do not panic or react in anger yourself.
- Be aware of where any weapons are stored; make sure

the person does not have easy access to weapons while experiencing rage.

- If the anger is short-lived and you feel safe, walk away or keep a distance and give the person space to calm down; listen or talk quietly if appropriate.
- Keep important numbers by the phone:
  - Police Emergency: 911 or your local emergency line
  - National Domestic Violence Hotline: 1-800-799-SAFE (1-800-799-7233)
  - Child Abuse Hotline: 1-800-4-A-Child (1-800-422-4453)
  - Suicide Hotlines: Hopeline: 1-800-SUICIDE (1-800-784-2433) or Suicide Prevention Lifeline: 1-800-273-TALK (1-800-273-8255)
  - Numbers for your local chaplain, doctor, or other professional

Controlling anger in the moment:
- Tell yourself to calm down; take deep breaths.
- Take a time out; move away from the situation; use the time to calm down, not justify your anger.
- Use a distraction, such as counting to ten, getting dressed, or singing a song.

Managing anger in the long term:
- See a professional; you will learn about anger management and determine if the anger is a symptom of another issue.
- Learn the source of and what triggers the anger so you can help avoid it, resolve it, or control it as appropriate.
- Exercise; find an appropriate physical release every day.
- Get enough sleep.

Anxiety

The physical symptoms of anxiety are caused by the brain sending messages to the body to prepare for the "fight or flight" response. The heart, lungs, and other parts of the body work faster. The brain also releases stress hormones, including adrenaline.

The following symptoms can occur as a result of an anxiety attack:
- rapid heartbeat or palpitations
- tightness or pain in chest
- shortness of breath, difficulty breathing, or feeling as though you can't get enough air
- dizziness, lightheadedness
- frequent urination
- difficulty swallowing
- nervousness, shaking, sweating
- hot flashes or sudden chills
- tingling in fingers or toes ("pins and needles")
- abdominal discomfort
- dry mouth
- insomnia
- irritability or anger
- inability to concentrate
- feeling unreal and not in control of your actions
- terror that is almost paralyzing
- feeling of dread

Anxiety attacks usually last five to ten minutes.

Places, activities, or circumstances frequently avoided by people who are managing anxiety include:
- shopping malls
- department stores
- restaurants
- religious service facilities (church, temple, etc.)

- meetings
- classrooms
- driving
- being alone
- airplanes
- elevators

What you can do if you have an anxiety attack:
- Breathe slowly to physically relax your body.
- Remind yourself of why you are safe.
- Learn and use relaxation techniques.
- Exercise daily.
- Think about if the anxiety or panic feelings have a pattern; learn your triggers.
- Talk to other people; join a support group.
- See a doctor or counselor.

Depression

Feeling depressed, sad, or stressed is a natural reaction to many of the life events and situations that arise during deployment and reunion. Clinical depression is when these feelings are out of proportion to the events or continue longer than a healthy amount of time. People with depression experience many of the following for prolonged periods:
- feelings of sadness, helplessness, hopelessness, worthlessness
- difficulty making decisions, remembering, or concentrating
- loss of interest and energy; lethargy
- difficulty sleeping or staying awake
- significant weight loss or gain
- increased isolation
- unusual fear or anxiety

- relationship problems with partners, friends, family, colleagues
- thoughts of death, suicide
- feelings of excessive guilt
- increased use of alcohol or drugs

There are many different circumstances that can ignite depression. A common one is grief. We naturally feel grief at the death of a someone close to us or at the breakdown of a marriage or other important relationship. That grief is a healthy reaction to a stressful life event. However, if the grief is severe and continues beyond a reasonable time, discuss your feelings with a doctor or counselor as it can easily lead to depression.

Some people experience symptoms of depression when they start or stop a medication. Service members may receive medications for a variety of reasons during deployment or at the beginning of reunion. Be sure to tell your doctor about any changes to medications in the past several months.

High levels of stress combined with poor eating and sleeping habits, no exercise, and other unhealthy lifestyle issues for prolonged periods can also trigger depression. Make it a priority to take care of your own basic physical needs.

Treatment for depression often combines "talking" therapy with a counselor, antidepressant medications to help chemically balance your brain, and natural therapies such as exercise, massage, and relaxation techniques. Many of the symptoms of depression are similar to other conditions, but treatment may vary so it is important to get a professional diagnosis and treatment plan.

In addition to formal treatment, you can help yourself deal with depression when you follow these guidelines:

- Set realistic goals and priorities.
- Break large tasks into small ones.
- Be around other people.
- Participate in activities you enjoy.

- Take care of yourself—eat well, exercise, sleep.
- Talk about major changes or decisions with others who know you well and can help you look at the situation objectively; postpone important decisions if possible until after the depression improves.
- Let your family and friends help you.
- Give it time.

Post-Traumatic Stress Disorder

PTSD is a complex health condition that can develop in response to a traumatic experience—a life-threatening or extremely distressing situation that causes a person to feel intense fear, horror, or a sense of helplessness.

It is important to know that you do not need to have actually been in a combat situation to have PTSD and that it affects people of all ages and ranks. "I see PTSD cases across the board from privates to colonels," says Col. Bob Stewart, chief of the Department of Behavioral Health at Fort Belvoir, Virginia. Individuals who spend most of their deployment "inside the wire" but who are exposed to death and trauma in medical settings, or who have experienced near-misses from mortars, RPGs, or other explosives, are also at risk of PTSD.

PTSD can manifest within days or take years to emerge. "Victims of other traumatic experiences, such as rape, are usually quicker to diagnose. When they relive the trauma, it is not the norm for their daily life so it usually stands out immediately," Col. Stewart explains. "In combat situations, after a trauma has occurred, we send our troops right back into the environment in which the trauma was experienced. If someone is having trouble processing what has happened, they might tell their battle buddies that they are hitting the rack early or taking some time to themselves. Avoidance symptoms are coping mechanisms to deal with the next day and are largely accepted by others within that environment. But when the soldier returns home, the symptoms are not typically accepted by spouses and others. Suddenly, it's a different environment and that's often when the realization of what has happened starts to catch up with the combat veteran. It often takes service members between six months and two years before they seek treatment for PTSD. A smaller percentage of service members come in for treatment within six months of their return from deployment, but these are frequently the most severe cases. The soldier tries to manage his symptoms on his own at first. He or she usually comes in when there is a realization that the symptoms aren't going away or they're getting worse, or a spouse or parent has told the soldier to get help."

The military also tries to screen for those who may be at higher risk. While each service branch is slightly different, Col. Stewart says that, in general, "Upon their return, service members complete a computerized form. They complete a similar questionnaire three months, six months, and one year later. It includes questions such as 'During the deployment, were you wounded, injured, assaulted, or otherwise physically hurt?' and 'Do you have a health concern stemming from…a blast or motor vehicle accident?' We then screen these responses to determine whether it is likely this person will be at risk for PTSD."

Common symptoms of PTSD:
- hyperarousal, always on guard
- nervousness
- easily startled
- anxiety symptoms such as sweating, shaking, rapid heartbeat and breathing
- haunting, unwanted recollections or flashbacks to the threatening experience
- withdrawal, emotional distance from other people
- problems with intimate relationships
- problems sleeping, nightmares
- changes in appetite

- difficulty concentrating
- loss of interest in work and activities; quality of work drops
- no longer wishing to attend religious services
- irritability
- depression
- headaches, stomachaches, dizziness, flu-like symptoms
- loss of memory
- survivor guilt
- unexplained anger or rage
- overuse of alcohol, drugs, or other addictions
- feeling of being trapped when in crowds or gatherings; always looking for the exit
- suicidal feelings and thoughts

A trigger is a reminder that activates anxiety, fear, flashbacks, and other symptoms of PTSD. Common triggers include:

- sudden loud noises
- people sitting, walking, or driving closely behind
- discomfort standing out in the open
- nightfall
- crying children
- large crowds
- long lines, waiting
- feeling disrespected
- sitting in traffic
- being in enclosed spaces, not seeing a way out
- hearing news about the war or about deaths
- seeing vehicles or people that remind you of where you were
- certain smells, weather, or other sensual reminders of an event

- going to drill, using weapons, military training
- being scheduled for deployment or a similar assignment

Managing PTSD in the long term:

To effectively manage PTSD, meet with a professional to create a treatment plan that works for you. Also:

- Take care of yourself—exercise regularly, get proper nutrition, sleep.
- Learn and practice stress coping and relaxation techniques.
- Make time for yourself; take "me time" without feeling guilty.
- Talk to a trusted friend.
- Join a support group.
- Write down your thoughts and feelings.
- Take a break from the news.
- Listen to music, play with pets, and do other activities you enjoy.
- Revisit an old hobby.
- Attend religious services.
- Don't compare yourself with others; everyone reacts differently to traumatic experiences and takes a different amount of time to process and heal.
- Avoid using alcohol or drugs.
- Be aware of your triggers.
- Accept help from others.
- Set goals and take one step at a time to reach them.

Helping a loved one with PTSD:

If you are a parent living away from your service member son or daughter, you can help identify issues:

- Trust your instincts. If you feel something is wrong, it probably is. Don't be afraid to ask the hard questions. This is still your child.

- Talk frequently; pay attention to conversations that seem out of the ordinary.
- Encourage your loved one to talk with a professional.
- If you are concerned, try to see your child in person. Fly him home for a weekend or get to where he is, if possible. He may be scared and trying to hide this.
- Let the unit chaplain or primary contact know your concerns. If you don't have these phone numbers they will be online—do a Web search.

What you can do if your loved one has an anxiety attack or disturbing flashback at a ball game, grocery store, or other public place:

- Show your loved one it is safe.
- Gently lead him or her away from the source of the panic or the trigger of the flashback.
- Show or lead your loved one to an exit.
- If in a car, roll down the window or pull over.
- Offer reminders of things that bring your loved one joy.
- Be patient, stay with him or her and offer appropriate comfort.

Ways you can help your loved one reduce and manage the symptoms of anxiety, depression, or PTSD:

- Keep regular exercise and sleep routines, eat healthy meals, and create an environment that makes it easy for your loved to do the same.
- Talk with a professional.
- Learn more about the prescribed treatment and coping strategies so you can be supportive.
- Don't take it personally.
- Reduce your own stress.
- Remember to laugh and have fun; do activities you both enjoy.

Kara Kitchen-Glodgett (wife):

Our son Wyatt, age six, still had anxiety issues a year after his dad came home. He went back into therapy to help with his worries. It was hard when he went back to school in the fall. For the whole first year of reunion, it was hard to get a babysitter and go out as a couple.

Linda Bong (wife):

Our son Bruce has separation disorder from being split up in two foster homes. It took three to four years to get a bond with us, although he immediately bonded with his sister Anna, who has Down Syndrome. It's hard for him to trust anyone again. He was lost when his dad left, now he is worried who else will leave him. Bruce wouldn't talk with his dad on the phone during the deployment; that was hard on Daryl. Within the first month Daryl was home, we hit a low. Anna said, "Dad, go back to the airport, go back to war." Months after homecoming, Bruce still didn't want to believe Dad was staying. He acted out, angry, thinking that Dad will leave again. It took four months before he started bonding again. Daryl had to learn to back off, learn how they had changed during the year.

Daryl had his own challenges, too. He got help for PTSD within the first two months. He had many sleepless nights. He didn't care if he lived or died. His counseling included how to live like a civilian again.

The counselor's advice for us was to put ourselves together first. We need to go to church, make time for family. Every day at 6 p.m. is our family hour. We have to make sure we leave work and other stuff behind. It has helped us bond with the kids. Daryl took three months off before going back to work so he could get himself and our family together. He was a nurse before deploying. But he found when he got back that he needed to keep moving. So he took a local truck driver job.

Kid Stress

Kids show stress in many different ways. They may show extreme aggression or withdrawal, disturbed sleep, clinginess, separation anxiety, anger, real fear or panic attacks. They may develop nervous habits such as nail biting or excessive eye blinking, or regress to earlier behaviors such as bedwetting.

If your child exhibits concerning behavior, ask your pediatrician for an evaluation or referral.

It has taken a year for us to feel normal again, but it really can never be the same. You can't go back. You just learn to live on.

Marla York (girlfriend):

Troy and I had been having some trouble before the deployment but we were trying to work it out. A few months into the deployment, he sent me an email saying he didn't want to work it out anymore. Our son Rodney (age six) felt abandoned. He emailed his dad every day, but Troy rarely answered. Rodney had nightmares about his dad being killed in Iraq. Rodney began talking with a counselor three or four times a month. He also talked with my daughter (age twenty-six) whose dad had died when she was five. To him, not having his dad there temporarily was very similar to having him die. We are going to work it out. In the end Troy decided we are best as a family.

Trisha Olson (wife):

I thought when Thad came home, it would be less stressful, but it wasn't. For months I was still doing most of the work I had been doing while he was gone. I worried about how he and the kids were adjusting and how to incorporate Thad back into our lives. Instead of worrying about him dying in combat, I worried about him being in a car accident. I worried about the irony of life, the things that come when you aren't looking anymore. I felt like I had to always be looking out for what might happen to us next.

I cried more often and felt even less in control than while he was gone. Every day was one big anxiety attack. I started talking with a therapist just so I had an outside person looking at my fears and helping me be rational. She helped me take things in steps and to see the bigger picture. I still have some fears to work out. I think part of that is the military way of life. It has been almost a year now and things in our house feel a little more balanced. I'm not looking forward to the next deployment, which I know will come sooner rather than later.

Margaret Coverly (wife):

My husband came home emotionally dead, unable to care about people he used to be so close to. After a few months of thinking the problem was me or our relationship, he talked with our chaplain who encouraged him to see a doctor. He is now being treated for depression. He is on medications that help balance things inside that he doesn't otherwise have control over. We had both changed so much through the deployment, we thought maybe we really weren't in love anymore. But it seemed so wrong to throw away twelve great years of marriage. It has been almost a year now of working at it, but things are improving day by day. My advice to others is to try not to take it personally, not to feel like it is your job to make him happy—he has to do that himself, and to keep looking until you find a doctor or therapist your husband is comfortable with. It takes one day at a time.

Gabriela Zupan (mom):

We are fortunate that our son has always been pretty open with us and stays in contact well. After he came home from Iraq there were multiple stressors in his life (car broken into, social security number stolen, an insurance fraud lawsuit, back surgery), so I'd been concerned for some time about how he could handle all of this so soon after the stress of war. For about a month before what I would call "a nervous breakdown" (the diagnosis is depression and anxiety) he was calling us sometimes three times a day, and did the same with his grandparents and sister. In retrospect I realize he was scared and needed to hear our voices. I noted increased drinking and finally he admitted to me that he'd been holing up in his apartment and weeping for weeks. He was on the rifle range that week, and that was when alarm bells went off loudly. I asked him if he was considering harming himself or others. He replied that he had considered

Benefits of Talking with a Chaplain

Chaplain Randy Imhoff:

Chaplains can be good listeners. Sometimes that is all that is needed, a listening ear.

They also have a unique position when it comes to confidentiality. The clergy/penitent privilege is a big plus when talking to a chaplain. What is discussed with the chaplain stays between the counselee and the chaplain.

Also, chaplains have a unique perspective in that they address issues from the spiritual standpoint. The spiritual aspect is just as important as the physical and mental aspects. This can help to heal the whole person.

Chaplains can also be great advocates and resources to find specific help with problems. Chaplains cannot solve every problem, but they can help people find the best resource to get help.

"maiming himself." This was so completely out of character for him! I searched the Web until I found the official Web site for the base where he's stationed. The Web site listed phone numbers. All I could think of was the chaplain. I called our son back with the number and gave him the option of either he called, *now*, or I would. He did, and within minutes he was being set up with mental health. He was evaluated the next morning. By that afternoon we had flown his sister down to stay with him for the week. She stayed by his side through the entire process and made sure he pursued help. For counseling, he was very uncomfortable talking to a man in the military, so we paid for a psychologist out in town, who was a woman, and where he felt most comfortable. He admitted that he just could not talk this out in front of a man, due to embarrassment.

Amy Palecek (wife):
When Peter first came home, he did not want to wear his Combat Medical Badge. It was too painful for him to answer questions about what he did to get it. Peter was a first shift lead medic at the level two trauma center. He ran the MASCAL the day of the glass factory bombing. But the day he got the Combat Medical Badge was actually the day he was running late to the showers. A mortar hit just minutes before he got there. A Marine was blown up and then Peter was there picking up the body parts. That day he knew he would need counseling when he came home. Now, after a few months at home, he has answered most of people's questions at work and he does wear the badge.

One morning about a month after he came home, we were in the middle of our normal morning commotion, getting our three-year-old ready and getting ready for work. Peter just stopped. He sat on the couch and when I asked him what was wrong, he said, "All I see is blood." Then he came out of it and went about his day. It was the first time since

being back that he had put on his uniform. He had already
been to the VA. He has hearing loss and needs orthodics and
one day he asked for a counselor. It was that easy to get an
appointment. He is not willing to talk with a military counselor; his counselor is a civilian at the VA satellite clinic. His
main concern is the nightmares. It's hard for anyone to sleep
in our house right now to begin with. We have a newborn
and then our three-year-old comes in each night to check
that Dad is still there. Then you add nightmares.

Peter works for the Northeast Counter Drug Program, a
joint Air and Army Guard program. Before the deployment,
he worked surveillance with the police force. Now he does
ion scans on money to test for drugs and use it as evidence in
court proceedings. Because of not only his work in Iraq but
also what he does for a living normally, one of the
assignments the counselor gave him is to practice observing
people when he is out in town. He is supposed to see that
90% of the people are good, not bad. So far he seems happy
with the counseling.

This is hard on the service member, but it's also hard on
the family. I have compassion fatigue from my work with the
family assistance center. We had a number of deaths in the
area and I have seen too many flags passed to families to
count. When Peter first deployed, I was angry and bitter and
felt like he was doing this to me. Then I felt like it was being
done to us both. Once I stopped being the victim, it was
easier to make it better for myself. It's important for the
family members to have a network. I have five other women I
met through a dysfunctional FRG. My husband calls us the
Crazy Wives Club. He recognizes how much we still need
each other. We have just as much to talk about and deal with
now that our husbands are home. You need friends and faith,
some way to not feel alone and know that someone else
understands what you are going through.

Boyce Folliot (soldier):

I had a very difficult time being close to people in any setting. After talking with my doctor about all of my symptoms—it's important to tell all your symptoms since one or two can mean many things—she diagnosed me with PTSD. I am now in treatment and it is tough but we are working through it. I am sorry for hurting my wife, Amelie. I try to tell her it is not her, but me. Our advice for other couples is to remember that what you have been through is not a normal circumstance of marriage. It is most likely the environment and events and what they did to your subconscious rather than anything that did or did not happen between you as a couple. Also, marriage counseling is good, but sometimes it's a different issue that an individual has to face before you can get together again as a couple. After I began treatments, we started "dating." We decided to treat it as a new relationship and take baby steps to get to know each other again and try to create some intimate situations that I feel comfortable with. It was too much pressure to feel like I had to live up to our wonderful eight-year marriage before the deployment. We both decided the past was great but we're not living in the past so we'll start new for the future and build a new and different relationship that can eventually be great in its own way.

Mariline Sanchez (mom):

My son attempted suicide twice before being diagnosed with PTSD. I am his mother and I feel so helpless. I can tell him he is a good young man and life is worth living. But things happened to him that make it hard for him to think straight about that. He doesn't even want to go to church anymore. He has a hard time accepting help from a professional. I am concerned not only about my son but other young men coming home from war. They are the future of our country and this is not a good way for them to start out their adult life. The stories are everywhere. Just type in PTSD in Google and you see newspaper reports of veterans everywhere coming home with all kinds of trouble. The military can't expect them to self-diagnose. Everybody should be required to go to a counselor for a year—that way nobody feels bad because everybody is doing it and then we help everybody. I would give my tax dollars for that. Look what these troops have done for me, for all of us. It's the least we can do for them.

Samantha Miles (soldier):

I was a postal clerk in Baghdad and also worked in the hospital for a while. As an admin assistant, I worked two weeks at a time in different locations as needed. It involved a lot of convoys and helicopter rides.

When I came home, I had a ten-minute medical evaluation. Then I changed duty stations to another post where my evaluation did not continue. I was selected for recruiter duty. That job requires a psych evaluation and certain issues came up that maybe weren't there when I first came home. I was having night terrors and in the middle of the day I had flashbacks. That evaluation led me to a military support group for PTSD. We meet every Wednesday at 1300. My husband wasn't for the support group at first. He thought we could work it out at home, pray about it.

I am a boxing fanatic. But the first match we went to, the crowd was rowdy. I was on the floor, crying. My husband had to carry me out. That's when my anxiety really started. It was too much for me to take in at once.

Many things began to affect me. I get a cold sweat and feel trapped in heavy traffic, especially if I can't see an exit. I have to sit facing open doors so I can see the way out. I don't like malls—too many doors. Someone is always walking toward me or behind me. I can't watch the news. Thunder storms are the biggest thing. They remind me of incoming mortar rounds. And to think about redeployment is out of the question.

At first, the doctor gave me sleeping pills and other meds. But my body rejected that. I knew I needed to deal with it. I am one of two females in the PTSD support group. At first I felt like my story was nothing compared to the men in the group who had experienced direct combat. But I've learned a lot about what other things affected me. Two female soldiers were killed when our shower trailer was hit. I was sad at the time, but the mission could not stop. Now those are the faces I see in my dreams, or I see the faces from the hospital.

Before the deployment, I was very organized and a great worker. Since then, my motivation has gone downhill. It seems like I have so much on my plate and it doesn't get done. It has affected my military performance and my combat readiness. I can't be near a weapon. It makes me cry; that seems to be my way of reacting, even though it doesn't make me feel better. If I'm not combat ready, I can't be in the military.

I'm twenty-eight years old. No one can ever prepare you for this. The military gave us a thirty-day combat stress course. It is nothing compared to what we went through. As much as the military tries to do, it's very hard if they haven't been there themselves. It's hard for me to be receptive to some of the counselors because they haven't been deployed and now they are telling me how I should feel.

Talking with the other soldiers in the support group helps me. They share stories, how they cope, relaxation techniques. Even though we have different experiences, we all have similar problems to deal with. One of the best things I've learned is to take time for myself—just ten or fifteen minutes of "Samantha time." I go sit in a corner or go to my room, shut the door, and lie down.

I've been in the support group for about nine months. My husband is now very supportive. He's seen the transition.

I did have a bout for two weeks in between that was worse, but I've made a lot of progress. When I come home from the group, he can see the sigh of relief and my muscle tension is gone. I don't know what I would do without my husband. He has been very tolerant of it all.

He tells me that I am not the woman he married. My own mother does not recognize me. I am withdrawn and don't like to do fun things that we used to. I'm probably afraid that those things will trigger anxiety. I do want to get back to being that person again. I'm really trying. I am taking a college course again, concentrating on one class to see if I can do it. I am eight classes away from my bachelor's degree. I haven't been back to college for three years because of the deployment and its effect on me. I want to be a high school English teacher. I believe that everything happens for a

---

Advice for Loved Ones of Someone with PTSD

Samantha's husband has been crucial in helping her deal with PTSD. She offers this advice for spouses:

My husband has known me all my life. I am very vocal. If I get quiet, he knows something is wrong and tries to address it right away. These are some of the things he does to help me:

- If I have an anxiety attack, he leads me to an exit.
- When there is traffic, he drives; he rolls down my window so I get fresh air. Sometimes he'll pull over so I can get out.
- When we are in a place like a mall, we walk as close as possible to the exit.
- When there is a storm, he gets on the floor with me and holds me.
- He tries to do more of the things I enjoy, slowly but surely getting us back to that.

reason. The Lord put me through what he did so I can have that understanding when I work with my students one day.

There are other ways I am helping myself. Military One Source is a very good group. They find civilian help for military members who don't want the military to know what's going on because of that stigma. I called them to help our marriage. I thought our marriage would suffer because of what I was going through. I would hate to lose my husband on top of it all. It is so important to have that support.

I go to physical therapy for my back and neck to relax my muscles. I have a ninety-minute massage every weekend—it's part of that Samantha time. I also attend a Healthy Thinking class one Tuesday a month. They teach us relaxation techniques to attack "the two-headed dragon." They teach us to get to the root of the problem, what the nightmare is the result of. I come home and share everything that I learn about coping with my husband so he benefits too. Men don't think they need support, but I think he does.

I've learned that a person can have these issues regardless of what job you had when you deployed. You don't need combat to have stress. No one can take care of you like you can. You have to take charge. You will have a life after the military. I realize that now and I'm working on it every day.

Chapter Four

Caregiving and Grief

As you reflect on and work through the challenges of this reunion, consider how you might be grieving what you've lost during the deployment. While your experience may have been rich with positive, life-changing events, you might also feel the loss of together time and missed memories. You might be coping with the injury or death of a loved one. The way you nurture and care for your relationships may also change during reunion.

Addressing the effects of caregiving and grief in a healthy, positive way will go a long way toward helping you begin to truly celebrate life once again.

Jolaine Barnes (wife):

Nothing was the same. We had lived these separate lives. During the deployment, I tried to keep so busy with classes and hobbies. I traveled with friends and created all these memories that Keefe wasn't part of. He missed it all. I found it so hard to talk about those memories with him, as if my joy would somehow hurt him. And he wasn't the same person when he came home. Some days I just wanted to go have fun again with my friends, where I didn't have to deal with whether or not he felt up to doing an activity. It was so confusing. I missed my life with Keefe, the way we were before the deployment. I missed the carefree time with my friends. Keefe felt lost, too, dealing with all the things that had happened in Iraq. We've had to really work at creating new memories together.

Sharon Prince (mom):

When we first learned of Henry's injuries, we didn't know what to expect. We spent three weeks at the hospital. When he was well enough, he was fitted for prosthetics and began physical therapy. The first several months, everyone was so focused on getting him mobile again. It was exhausting work. But the real work was what was happening in our hearts and souls. His life, our lives, were changed forever. And while blessed compared to many, Henry had to come to terms with how he would live this new life.

Melissa Mahlenbrock (wife):

Now that Dave is gone, it's hard to want to get up each day. It seems unfair to him for me to be happy. The hardest days are the days that should bring me joy. Kadence will do something new: her first birthday, learning to walk. I'm sad because I want Dave to see it, too. I don't know what I'd do if it weren't for Kadence. She is my reason for getting up each day.

Caregiver Perspective

You are a caregiver. During deployment, you are caring for a long-distance relationship with your deployed loved one. You are supporting people around you, some of whom don't understand what you are going through and don't know how to support you. You are caring for yourself during a stressful time. If you are a military spouse with children, you are playing the role of a single parent during the deployment.

Your deployed loved one is also a caregiver, keeping himself and others in the unit safe, caring for the people who benefit from the mission, and maintaining a long-distance relationship with family and friends back home.

Caregiving is tough work and takes a lot of emotional and physical energy. Think for a moment about a caregiver for someone who is very ill or elderly. In addition to a lot of time spent focused on the person she is caring for, that caregiver is also trying to maintain her own life and family, adjust schedules to accommodate the unexpected, renew her energy—which seems to quickly deplete, and deal with the changes taking place for the person in her care.

Take a moment to reflect on who you are taking care of, what you feel about those in your care, the ways being a caregiver depletes your energy and how the experience makes your life richer. Often thinking of yourself in this role helps you see from a different perspective.

Leaving a caregiving role or having it change significantly can also have a big impact on you emotionally and physically. No matter whether an illness or relationship improved or worsened during your care, you may question the decisions you made, regret how you spent your time, or simply be exhausted from the experience.

If you're a parent of a young service member, you may have had an active role in supporting your child's morale, storing belongings or taking care of finances during the deployment. Now, your child or a new spouse may be taking those responsibilities, leaving you feeling less helpful and involved. The frequency of your communication may change and your role as parent may become more like an adult friend to your son or daughter.

If you're a significant other, you are now working to rebuild your lifelong relationship and become closer as a couple. You may be worried about each other's health and well being after challenging circumstances or as you adjust to being together again. If you have children, your parenting role will now change again.

You may also have added a caregiving role, caring for your own or another service member's injuries or helping a loved one cope with stress or anxiety.

Some of the emotional attachments you made during the deployment will remain while others will change dramatically. There may be some people in your extended family, for example, who were there for you during the deployment even if they didn't always understand what you were going through. Some new friends in your family readiness group or other support group may have been your lifeline during the deployment and might now just disappear back into their own lives. Perhaps your relationship with neighbors or coworkers will change now that you have a different situation.

Service members also experience emotional attachments during deployment, with people at home who wrote to them, comrades in the unit, the people they were helping on their mission, and at some level with the people they were protecting against. Now they are leaving those behind to begin new attachments back home.

One effect of all this attachment and detachment and change in caregiver roles is grief. When you experience life and people more intensely, you miss them more when changed or gone.

Grief Perspective

Grief is the way a person responds to and works toward acceptance of a loss. There are many normal, everyday things you and your service member may grieve during deployment and reunion. You may grieve the temporary loss of your loved one during deployment, the everyday changes that took place during a deployment, lost time with a child or each other, missing out on what the other experienced, loss of innocence because of what you experienced during the deployment, or loss of your former life together. You may also grieve major events or changes in your life such as the transformation of a deployed child into an adult, the effects of a natural disaster, the loss of function or a limb due to injury, the death of a friend or family member, or the death of your service member.

When your life changes as it does during a deployment or reunion, you take some things with you in the next chapter of your life, but it's not the same. One of the biggest sources of grief for families in which everything else seems to have gone well is the fact that because of this deployment experience, life will never be the same. Everyone has changed. Roles, decision making, the way you each look at life—it's all changed by this experience. You can't simply rewind and go back to the way things were before.

Daily Life

For Joe Schmidt's wife, Erika, grief came from missing all the firsts with their five-year-old quadruplets while she was in Germany for a year. They did the best they could to keep Mom part of their daily lives and milestones. Joe shares, "She took her laptop computer with her, plus a webcam and headset. We set up times where the webcam was on. One time the kids and I were decorating Easter eggs. She observed and gave us instructions. The quadruplets also began kindergarten this year. So on the first day of school, the webcam was set up so that she could watch the kids get on the bus for the first time and they could wave goodbye to Mom from the bus. She shopped for their school supplies in Germany so she could be part of it."

Support System

If you have moved away from base during deployment, you may feel another loss when you move back because you are moving away from your current support structure.

Paige Shepherd shares, "During my husband's first deployment, I wanted to stay at the military post where he deployed from, which was in Colorado. But when Mark deployed a second time, I wanted to be home in Texas near family. My family is very close and we talk on a daily basis. For the first deployment, I knew I had to stay at Mark's post. I was nineteen years old and I had to learn to grow up and not depend on my parents. Army life was brand new to me, Colorado was new to me, living alone was new to me. I had to learn to appreciate these things. I also learned that sometimes being around the whole military thing all the time can really wear you down. You see soldiers all the time and wonder 'Why isn't my soldier here?' I gained my independence the first time around and I am so grateful. But the second time I knew I needed my family and friends around me, plus I was pregnant. My mom was really there for me when Mark could not be. I will go home again if he ever deploys again. The comfort of family really helps the morale. But when it came time to return to Fort Carson, it was very tough to leave my family in Texas. We all knew it was coming, but it gets hard to leave the people you love."

Natural Disaster

Sometimes grief is due to loss of physical possessions, changes to your home or job, or unexpected relocation.

In the hours before Hurricane Katrina struck, Mae Westerly drove from Gulfport, Mississippi, to Pensacola, Florida, with her three children, a week's worth of clothes and diapers, a mix of food from the cupboard, each child's special blankie, a box of important papers, and a box of family photos. They had evacuated before. But this time turned out to be different.

"You know it's a possibility and that's why you get out of town. But you really don't feel in your heart that you could lose everything," Mae says. Her husband? Deployed to Iraq. Her friends? A few made it to Pensacola, others scattered to stay with family in other states. "It took months to find everyone. I had their Mississippi contact information, but in most cases, I didn't know where they had evacuated to or if they got out safely." Most of her Gulfport friends' husbands were also in Iraq. Some were called to search and rescue duty, delaying their deployment to Iraq by about a month.

"It was so awful," Mae recalls. "Here we had lost our house, our belongings. And our husbands were over there rebuilding instead of here with us. It was hard to not be angry about the irony of it. Then one night, our five-year-old daughter, Grace, was saying her nightly prayers. She prayed, 'God, I miss my Polly Pockets and my books, but I am lucky I had those things. Please bring a toy and a book to all of the children in the world who don't have any.' I just cried and hugged her. How could I be angry at our situation? We had people around us; the people at Pensacola were so generous and helped us in whatever way we needed. Some kids in the world did not have that and my daughter got it. She really got it. From that day forward, I vowed to work through my self-pity by helping and praying for others."

Mae says that when her husband did return from Iraq, "We had the most intense reunion you can imagine. We had both lost so much, lived with so little for such a long time, had friends who died, children who were alive and so precious. There was nothing as important as being together and loving each other and our family. We grieved, how we grieved. But it was with an incredible appreciation for what we had left. Every moment we take as a blessing. If a disagreement begins to surface, we honestly just deal with it and quickly move on. You have to live each day, really live in the moment. And just love each other"

When a Loved One is Injured

Lori Zimney (mom):

Billie's Humvee got bombed. He was a gunner. It threw him on the ground. He was out for a while and lost his hearing for a short time. He thought it was nothing heroic, just got bombed, part of the job he had to do.

Keith (soldier):

I lost my right leg. I was in the rear vehicle of a convoy when an RPG (rocket propelled grenade) hit our truck. I have a new leg now. Technology is really amazing. I can physically function. But there are times I can feel my leg that was left in Baghdad.

Your loved one's injuries may be physical injuries, psychological changes, or spiritual wounds. It may take more than time to heal. It may take medical attention, years of working with experts to guide you, support from family and friends, and a deep well of faith and hope.

Tips from Families Who have Dealt with Injuries

Give the injured person space to realize what has happened and to begin grieving what has happened.

Sometimes it's tough for people to talk about themselves. An injured Marine shares, "It is tiring to talk about yourself...I am not used to that kind of talk. I want to talk to everyone, but not all at once."

Be there in whatever way they need.

Sharon Prince explains, "Henry needed medical care. Appointments, medications, rescheduled appointments. He also needed to know that we didn't love him any less. He is still a whole person who has so much to give the world. He wanted time for himself and time when we simply laughed. He needed to tell stories and have people around him who listened with great interest. He needed to know he had options, that he would be able to contribute his talents. He needed to feel like himself again. He wanted to feel like he had a normal life. And we had to learn how to focus on him and not his injuries all the time."

Look for options and outside support.

Wounded service members share a camaraderie that even other service members don't really share. They know firsthand the phantom pains on limbs that don't exist, the ache of healing bones, the fears about adapting to life and new jobs with their injuries. There are options for severely injured service members to begin their healing and recovery with others who are going through similar situations. Each branch of service has facilities that can help. There are also local support groups for service members as they assimilate back into regular jobs and life with their families.

Lt. Col. Timothy Maxwell suffered a serious head wound in Iraq. When he returned to the United States, he asked if he could use a building to help his wounded comrades get through the final phases of recovery together. The Marines at Maxwell Barracks deal with change-of-life issues and get individual counseling while recovering alongside people who understand what it's like, their fellow wounded warriors.

Emanuel Pierre and Stuart Contant, two Apache helicopter pilots who had trained together, deployed together with 101st Airborne Division, and then crashed together in Afghanistan, realized that while the rehabilitation from their injuries was painful, overcoming the mental hurdles would be an even longer process. They started a support group for wounded soldiers that meets twice a month at Blanchfield Army Hospital.

The Angels of Mercy program at Walter Reed is an example of many volunteer programs serving the needs of wounded service members and families. A young corporal who had received a holiday gift package expressed to those volunteers how much they meant to him. "I wanted to take this moment to thank you for your kind words sent to me while I was in Walter Reed Army Hospital in Washington, D.C. I was wounded in Iraq by an IED and suffered head trauma. My recovery has been swift and while I still have some lingering effects, I feel that I will make a complete recovery. Part of that is due to your support and prayers and I appreciate them more than you know. I am now home and will start college in the fall. I hope that your life is blessed with family and friends as is mine. Continue to pray for all of the soldiers who still serve in Iraq as well as Afghanistan and everywhere else in the world."

Take care of yourself.
You are no good to anyone else unless you are healthy and able to deal with daily responsibilities. Eat, sleep, exercise. Talk with others who understand what you are going through.

Keep the faith.
"The toughest part is the uncertainty and keeping your outlook positive," says Sharon Prince. "Family members need support too." Find a prayer partner or anything that helps your faith be a source of hope.

When a Loved One at Home Dies

Tamara Stanoch:

I can instantly put myself right back to the day that changed our lives. It was in the evening when we received the phone call. We were actually in the middle of a little spat. I answered the phone and when I heard Gordy's full name, Gordon Stanoch, I smiled a little and handed him the phone. I remember sitting in the basement thinking "Boy, he hates telemarketers; that serves him right." Only seconds later did it hit me that this was no telemarketer. He was being deployed. Here we were only moments earlier arguing about something I'm sure was nothing and now our family was going to be torn apart. Our son, Derek, had just turned two. I was nine months pregnant. I remember thinking, "How am I going to do this? How is Gordy going to be able to leave us? What about Derek? Daddy is his best friend."

From that evening on our days were filled with running all over. There was informing Gordy's job, informing the banks, informing family and friends, and not to mention informing our OB/GYN. My delivery date was moved up so Gordy could be there for the birth of our second child. The days prior were so hectic that we didn't have any ideas for a name. Grayce Marie was born May 12, 2004. Gordy boarded the bus to Camp Ripley on May 15, 2004. My mother took Derek to wave goodbye since I was still in the hospital. One can read the emotion in the pictures that were taken that day. Gordy's unit was held up for quite some time in Fort Dix, New Jersey. We were lucky our men and women were granted a number of leaves before leaving for Iraq, giving Gordy a total of ten days with Grayce. The leaves were nice but each time it got harder to say goodbye.

Just as we thought we might be okay, our lives became hell. It was a Saturday afternoon and I had just finished talking to Gordy on the phone. I still had the phone in my

hand when I walked into Grayce's room. I found Grayce
unresponsive and not breathing. Without hesitation I dialed
911. Our quiet home had now become full of rescue personnel. Grayce was taken to the hospital. They were not able to
resuscitate her. She passed away July 10th during her afternoon nap. We followed all the protocol in trying to have
Gordy found. Red Cross was notified by the chaplain. I am
not sure how long I waited before I finally made the call
myself. I reached Gordy at the movies on his cell phone. I
remember telling him to find someone near him and I had to
say the most dreadful words, "Gordy, something happened.
Grayce is gone." The phone was silent but I could tell Gordy
was running. He was running back to base. He ran into a
person who relayed the Red Cross message. Gordy flew home
the next morning. The next few days seem like a blur. It was
so unreal planning a funeral for our baby girl.

On the way to the wake, I asked Gordy what he thought
about going to back to Fort Dix. Before he could answer, I
told him I would stand behind him no matter what. Hearing
his decision to return was obviously harder than not to hear,
but we knew that was where he belonged. A couple days
before his return Gordy had been flipping through the phone
book calling anyone and everyone to see if there was somewhere for me to go for support. Gordy may not be aware of
this but while he was trying to take care of me, I was trying to
take care of him. I had contacted the major from his unit and
asked him to watch Gordy and encourage him to see the
chaplain.

Gordy's unit was once again granted a leave, so we got
to see Gordy again over Labor Day. Our third child was
conceived. I remember calling Gordy in the middle of the
night to tell him I was pregnant. You could tell he answered
the phone with some uncertainty and was relieved when I
said everything was okay. I told him he was going to be a

daddy again. You could hear him smile from the phone if that makes any sense.

The unit left for Iraq in early January. Thanks to today's technology our conversations were very frequent. He was able to be as active as possible through this pregnancy and also assisting me in grieving for Grayce. I kept a lot of the grieving away from our conversations. I wanted his mind to be kept focused on his mission and his safety. Gordy still doesn't talk much about Grayce, but there are little comments that let me know she is very much on his mind. One evening Derek looked up and said "Look, Mommy, Grayce's stars." He told me that Daddy told him that. Gordy told me that while traveling through Baghdad to their base, he saw a falling star and knew Grayce was watching over him. He believes that it was because Grayce was with him that he was not involved in or saw anything really bad. So we were given some comfort in our loss. We knew she was watching over her daddy, his very own angel.

Gordy was granted emergency leave in May for the delivery of our third child. Ella Grace was born May 20, 2005. That was the day that our healing started. Our conversations consisted of holding up Ella in front of the webcam while Derek bounced on the bed in back of us. Derek didn't talk to Daddy much. He would say he was too tired. I think it made him too sad. He would sit in front of the computer every now and then and make faces back and forth with Daddy.

Gordy returned home October 29, 2005 right before his favorite holiday. It is hard to believe that he has been back for almost a year. The past year has been filled with so much emotion. Gordy was finally home and safe. We knew we were going to be okay. Gordy didn't come home the same Gordy who left. He was a little more withdrawn at first. There were days it almost seemed like he forgot he was a husband and a daddy. Before Iraq, he never got angry. When he came home, the littlest things could set him off.

Because of his leave for Grayce's funeral, Gordy didn't have as much leave time accumulated so he returned to work November 28. He decided to leave his place of employment after almost nine years. His decision to leave has put him in a much better position and I am very happy to say that Gordy is doing much better. He is once again a great husband and the most wonderful daddy. He has joined me a couple times at our monthly SIDS meetings. During one of our meetings at the SIDS center, he did mention that it is very hard for him because when he left Grayce was a baby and when he returned Ella was no longer a baby. To this day Gordy remains pretty quiet about our loss of Grayce. The little comments still appear and he waters the grass at "her house" (the cemetery). So, I know she is very much a part of his thoughts and heart.

Derek is now four. He was forced into a whole new world and had to grow up fast. People will comment that he seems older than he is. At times those comments actually hurt because he didn't get to be the normal two and three year old. We have noticed a lot more angry outbursts lately. We have addressed this with his pediatrician. With the combination of both the loss of his dad for two years and the loss of his baby sister this may all be normal. We will keep close tabs on it. He still sees Grayce's stars. While most kids wonder where they come from, Derek wonders how babies get to heaven. He plays soccer in the cemetery, and he sends balloons to Grayce to play with. How much of her does he remember or will he remember, we don't know. We know that for as long as we are around he will know he has two sisters.

Ella Grace is now sixteen months old and wild as can be. She has many of Grayce's characteristics. The dimples, the beautiful smile, and the little giggle we got to hear from Grayce just a few times. We always comment that Grayce sent her to keep us busy. We know she is giggling up there in heaven.

As for me, I am forever changed. My life is now lived day by day. Adjusting to Gordy returning was a little challenging. You get accustomed to doing the things you want and when you want. There were times that plans were made and I realized I never informed Gordy. I noticed I became weaker when he returned. He was here to help me take care of the kids, leaving time for me to take in all that we had been through. It had been a year since Grayce had died and the tears still came out of nowhere and the pain was still as if it was the day we lost her.

Looking back at all of this, it makes me proud that we made it. There still are little struggles but nothing we can not overcome. With the help of family and friends we were able to make it through. Many of them went way beyond the call of duty. My parents sacrificed much of their lives to help me with the kids. Derek spent many days working alongside Grandpa in the garage. My mom became one of my best friends. A good friend from high school checked in on us. Another friend stopped by at least two days out of the week to make sure we were all okay. We met a lot of new wonderful people through our journey. Gordy made close friendships while he was away. Back home I attended a family support group through the military and made new friendships. I continue to attend monthly SIDS meetings where I have met the most wonderful people I wish I never would have had to meet. I believe in my heart we made it through because of our little angel Grayce Marie.

Katherine Leland:

We got pregnant with our first baby immediately upon Jacob's return and then lost the baby the day we went to hear the heartbeat, at thirteen weeks. We were and are devastated. The day we went to hear the heartbeat, we were actually scheduled to go on a relationship retreat that the Army was offering as part of the deployment experience. It's been the most difficult experience I have ever faced in my life. I thought when my husband deployed to go overseas that I would never get through it and then when he came back, our joy quickly turned to sorrow as we faced the loss of our baby. We have been struggling with grief and are so very lost.

Erin Plummer:

My best friend, Megan, was killed in a car accident one month after Jeff deployed. Jeff's unit was short staffed and even though we had all known each other since we were seven years old, Megan was not an immediate family member, so Jeff couldn't come home. It wasn't even going to the funeral without him that was the worst. I still didn't really believe it had happened at that point. But then at three months, and six months, and the one year anniversary. The times when I really missed her phone calls and lunches and walks and our talks. Going through that on my own without Jeff here was so hard on both of us.

When a Service Member Dies During Reunion

Laura Benita (mom):

It was Christmas vacation. Cory had been back in the States for three months. He and Jill and their new baby were staying with us for two weeks. The holiday was just as I pictured it. Our two daughters were also home from college. Cory's friends from the neighborhood were bustling in and out. We opened presents and ate good food. My husband, Charlie, had got a deer so we had venison and duck. It was perfect. The day after Christmas, Cory went out with some friends snowmobiling. He grew up in those woods so I didn't think anything of it. After worrying for more than a year of his deployment, I was trying to let myself worry less. Well, they got going too fast and Cory's sled didn't make the turn and he hit a tree. He went head over the sled. He died an hour later at the hospital.

When a Service Member Dies on Duty

Melissa Mahlenbrock (wife):

Dave and I first met when we were nine, fell in love at fourteen, and married immediately after my graduation from high school. He was one year older than me. He joined the Army and was stationed to Schofield Barracks, Hawaii. When he found out he would be sent to Iraq as early as December, I flew to Hawaii and we were married by a justice of the peace. We made a tape for each other saying how we felt about each other and saying goodbye. We wanted to be able to hear each other's voices during the deployment.

Dave was told he would not be able to have children. On January 21, 2004, he deployed to Iraq. Five days later, I found out I was pregnant. It was the same day he called to tell me he was okay and in Kuwait.

September 25, Dave came home on R&R leave, one week after our daughter Kadence was born. I was very nervous. I looked different—I had just had a baby! I had flown home to New Jersey to stay with my parents and have the baby there. So that's where Dave came on his leave. He took Kadence everywhere. She was only a week old, but he wanted to be her dad so he took her to the movies, the mall, the zoo, even Chuck E. Cheese. He made a DVD of himself reading bedtime stories to her. Even though it would be a while before she could watch it and understand, he wanted her to see him every night and hear his voice and know that he was there with her.

Dave was scheduled to come home from Iraq December 29. He was a combat engineer. On December 3, 2004, he was in the passenger seat of the first Humvee, on his way back from Kirkuk clearing a route for the convoys. They did this every Friday to get their supplies. An improvised explosive device detonated, killing Dave. The driver next to him lost both of his legs but is now doing well. A soldier in the back seat was unharmed. Dave always wore an armband with a picture of Kadence in it. He was thrown in the explosion and when they lifted his body, there was the picture of Kadence underneath him. Someone picked it up and sent it to me. It's all burned and very special.

Dave had been able to call me every day between 12:30 and 2:30. We would talk for a half hour. We were really lucky that way. I was about to have lunch that day. It was 2:30 and he hadn't called. My mom had gone to my sister's basketball game. Dad was in the basement getting Christmas decorations. The doorbell rang and I thought it was probably a package. I set Kadence in the bouncy seat and went to the door. I must have been looking down because what I remember seeing was shiny shoes. You just know instantly. I screamed really loud and my dad came running up the stairs. I passed out. When I came to, I was on the couch and the soldiers were telling my dad what had happened. They were very official and efficient. They left the notice and explained their duties and that they would be back the next day.

My dad didn't want to leave me, but he went to get my mom and pulled my sister out of the ball game. It was all a blur. I didn't believe it. My family was all there. They would ask me, "Do you know what happened?" I was very much in denial.

The soldiers did come back the next day. They showed me pictures of caskets and asked where Dave should be buried. Dave and I had discussed briefly what would happen if he died. He had life insurance. He wanted a military funeral. But that was about it. It's a hard conversation to have in detail.

That past July, Dave had written a letter for Kadence. He gave it to his sergeant in case anything happened to him. I received it a few days after he died. It said things like he would understand if I remarried. He told Kadence to listen to her mom and not to date until she's seventeen. He also said he wanted the song "American Soldier" to be played at his funeral.

Through Soldiers' Angels, Toby Keith's agent found out about our story. Toby called me in person. He dedicated "American Soldier" to Dave and sent me the handwritten lyrics in a frame with a note. There have been special things like that. Dave was one of the first soldiers in our area to die. I wanted everyone to know who he was. He is not a number. He is a hero.

We were only married for a year and three months, most of which we spent apart. But from age nine, we had known we would be best friends for life. The fact he was gone didn't hit me for a couple months. I bought a house in New Jersey and decorated it how Dave would like it so if he came home it would feel like home to him. Even now, almost two years later, I can't sleep. Something cute will happen and I can't wait to tell him. Each day, 2:30 comes and he hasn't called. Everything reminds me of him.

I want Kadence to know her dad. I talk about him all the time. Kadence knows who Daddy is from pictures. She sleeps with a teddy bear that has his picture on it. She watches the DVD of him reading every night. She makes him cards and I put them in a shoe box so she'll have them one day, these things she made for her dad. We have pictures of him every-where. I framed and hung his awards. He died doing what he loved and I am so proud of him.

This past June, my parents moved to North Carolina. Dave and I always wanted to live near my parents. So I sold my house in New Jersey and moved to North Carolina, too. In Dave's letter, he told Kadence that Grandpa needs to meet all her boyfriends. That will be easier if we're close by!

Dave is buried in Arlington. I chose that because I realized through this experience that I can't control the future. I don't know where I'll be. And he deserves to be there. It's an honor. We make the seven-hour drive on his birthday in August and on December 3. I plan to do something here, though, that we can have when we can't get to Arlington and want a special place. A memorial garden or a bench. A place for me to go and for Kadence to play in and feel near her dad.

We have come a long way. The VA was helpful for all the official stuff, the actual benefits. And TAPS [Tragedy Assistance Program for Survivors] has been great. We get together every May and it's good for us all to be there with others who have gone through this. I tried a widow's group here. But they were all at a point where they could laugh. I would tell my story and they would cry. I can't cry yet. Someone told me when I start to cry I'll start to heal. Sometimes it is hard for me to relate to some of the other widows. At twenty-one, I am always the youngest.

I write things down in my journal. And when it seems like I haven't made any progress, I read what I've written. Then I can see the changes. I am getting better even if I don't feel it. It's there in my journal, in my own handwriting, my own advice. And I have my family.

My mom said, "You had to grow up so fast."

Jackie Finney (wife):

"When they came to tell me Mac had died, I threw up on the carpet. At the time Mac was being killed, I had been up late cleaning the carpet and now I was puking on it. Our son Jason is nine. He came home from school that day talking about the World Series and excited to go play ball with his friends. He ran in and out. Heather, she is six, talked and talked about the lady who brought a snake to school that day. I let them go on with their world another couple of hours, their happy world. While I sat there thinking about how to tell them our worst fears were real. How to say we'll be okay. How to believe it myself so they would trust my words.

Notifications

Each service branch has a slightly different protocol for delivering the news of an injury or death. The procedures are meant to ensure expeditious and personal notification.

In the event of a service member's injury or illness, only the primary next of kin will be notified and it may be by phone. In all death and missing cases, the primary next of kin and secondary next of kin, as well as any other person listed on DD Form 93 (Record of Emergency Data) will be notified.

Whenever possible, the notifier's grade is equal to or higher than the grade of the casualty. When the primary next of kin is also a service member, the notifier's grade will be equal to or higher than the grade of the primary next of kin. In general, personal notification will be made between 6 a.m. and 10 p.m. local time. The primary next of kin is always notified first.

Although procedures vary, the process generally follows notification of the primary next of kin and secondary next of kin as soon as possible, usually within twenty-four to forty-eight hours. For minor injuries, the hospital or service member may call. For seriously injured or very seriously injured cases, the primary next of kin is usually notified by phone. For deaths, notification is in person.

Primary next of kin is determined by relationship to the service member, in this order: spouse, children, parents, guardians, siblings, grandparents, other relatives. It is important for the service member to keep the Record of Emergency Data updated with next of kin information, including correct contact information. Also, if the next of kin will be out of the area for any time, it is important to leave a contact number with the rear detachment commander or family readiness contact to avoid notification delays.

For seriously and very seriously injured service members, the primary next of kin may be issued Invitational Travel Orders. Transportation and lodging may be offered for up to three immediate family members in two-week increments to allow family to be near the injured service member to aid in recovery. Families are housed in hotels, military guest lodges, or a Fisher House if available. A Fisher House is located within walking distance of major military and VA medical centers.

The Traumatic Injury Protection Insurance (TSGLI) benefit provides financial assistance to service members during their recovery period from a serious traumatic injury.

Wounded service members have case managers assigned to work with them during their recovery. These individuals assist the member and family with information about medical evaluations, veteran service organizations, and programs offered through chaplains, social workers, and Family Assistance Centers.

Please see the appendix for some of the many Department of Defense, government agency, and nonprofit organizations with programs to support injured service members and their families as well as benefits and grief support for families whose service member has died.

Stacy Westbrook (wife):

When soldiers were killed from our base, I went to the memorials. My husband knew them. I wanted to go for him, even though it was so hard. I brought back something, like a memorial card, to remind him of knowing them and to feel like he was there. I am so appreciative of their sacrifice. I went out of respect, but it was very difficult. It could have been him.

Common Symptoms of Grief

The way you respond to loss depends on many things, such as the circumstances of the loss or death, previous experiences with similar losses, your age and relationship to the person, and other things that are going on in your life at the time.

After a sudden traumatic loss, you may experience shock, disbelief, numbness, helplessness, and disorientation. You may find it hard, even after months, to stop replaying the circumstances of the death. It may be difficult to sleep or to concentrate. You may experience physical symptoms, such as exhaustion, muscle aches, trouble digesting food, or difficulty healing a physical injury. You may also have bouts of anger or feel guilty or discouraged about your role in the event. Existing illnesses can worsen or new conditions may develop. More serious emotional reactions may include anxiety attacks, chronic fatigue, depression, or thoughts of suicide.

Grief may be intensified by major life adjustments that come with a loved one's death, such as parenting alone, adjusting to single life, returning to work, working through financial changes, or helping another person grieve.

You may also find it difficult to grieve other losses while you are grieving this one. Less than two years after my husband died, my dad died of a heart attack. For a long time, I couldn't grieve my father's death. He was sixty-four. Though still young, he had lived twenty-six years longer than my husband. I was still grieving the loss of my life partner. Even though I missed my dad, I didn't feel anything about his death until months later when I looked through old pictures from my childhood. Even then, it all seemed out of order.

The "natural order of things" is one reason it is difficult for parents to cope with the death of a child. We think a parent is supposed to die first. When a partner dies, it is disorienting for both older widows, who have spent their life with this person, and for young widows, whose life with their partner was just beginning.

Everyone going through a loss sees it from an individual point of view based on their relationship and where they are in life.

Often when you are grieving, you have a heightened awareness of others' suffering. When you hear of natural disasters, it might be more than you can bear to think about the people affected because you have joined an unwanted club of people who know what grief really is.

Symptoms of grief usually lessen after a few months. Some grief experts believe that with intentional effort and time, you can completely heal and move on to a happy life. Others believe you don't ever stop grieving; you find ways to better manage your grief. You may find that thoughts and feelings about the person come and go. The anniversary of the loss or a special day such as a birthday or holiday can remind you of the person. Places, people, time of day, events, smells, and sounds can all be reminders. Even years later, your grief may resurface when faced with financial decisions, new relationships, and other life changes.

What happens in grief may surprise you. Days, months, and sometimes years after the loss, you may experience:

- difficulty accepting the death; expecting your loved one to come home again
- short-term memory loss
- aches and pains, fatigue
- heightened emotions, such as anger, irritability, or anxiety
- crying easily
- comparing your situations with others
- lack of self-confidence
- questioning who you are now and what you should be doing
- disturbed eating and sleeping habits
- feeling overwhelmed
- reliving the event

- strong feelings of longing for your loved one
- feeling like part of you has also died
- guilt that you couldn't do something to keep your loved one from dying
- regret over things said or unsaid
- depression
- change in priorities; things that were once important may not matter so much anymore
- questioning your beliefs

Working Through Grief

Each person grieves differently. Give yourself permission to find your own way. A few things you can do to help yourself grieve:

- Allow yourself to grieve.
- Take good care of yourself: eat well, sleep, exercise.
- Tell your doctor about your loss and how you are coping.
- If you have trouble remembering things, carry a small notebook and write them down.
- Spend time among friends; do things you enjoy.
- Find a trusted friend or chaplain you can talk to.
- Create a ritual, such as sending up balloons on birthdays and anniversaries, visiting a grave site, attending a prayer service.
- Think of a death anniversary as a birthday into heaven.
- Write down your thoughts and feelings.
- Remind yourself that each person grieves differently.
- Be kind to yourself.
- Allow yourself the time to reflect.
- Recall positive memories, write down memories or collect photos that remind you; create a memory book

or other keepsake that helps you remember this person's life and not just the person's death.

- Listen to children; they have an amazing wisdom about God and the afterlife.
- Donate money or volunteer time to an organization in honor of the person.
- Do not use alcohol or drugs to self-medicate your feelings.
- Create a place in your home or another favorite place where you can think about your loved one, be with and talk with your loved one in a special way, and honor that person's memory.
- Be patient; it takes time to accept what's happened.
- Don't dwell on whether or not there is something you could have done to change what happened; it has happened.
- Don't wonder why it didn't happen to you instead; it didn't.
- Know that your loved one would not want you unhappy; choose to celebrate the life you live now.
- Read about others who have experienced loss, talk with others, learn about grieving; know that you are not alone.
- Appreciate the people who are still in your life; tell them you love them.
- Take what you've learned from this and make it easier next time; talk about what you want for your loved ones when you die, learn what they want to happen when they die.
- Keep the faith.
- Go at your own pace and make your own decisions about when to donate clothing, whether or not to wear wedding rings, and other personal changes.
- Take it one step at time.

When Someone You Know Has Lost a Loved One

"Any family that has lost a loved one will be in shock for weeks.
Follow up months later and make sure they are taking care of
themselves. People look at those things the first days and weeks
and then think they are okay. But when other people are getting
used to the idea of this person being gone, the spouse and parents
are just realizing what happened." — Amy Palecek

What you can do to help someone who is grieving:

- Listen.
- Don't try to make it better with comments about it
  being "for the best" or implying the person will "get over
  it" or that "life will go on"; don't suggest that a loved one
  can be replaced with another spouse or child someday.
- Offer practical help, such as babysitting, cooking,
  running errands, doing chores, or writing thank you
  notes; don't make your offer too broad—saying "if there
  is ever anything I can do" can be too overwhelming for
  a person who is grieving to respond to or act on.
- Watch for signs of depression or other serious issues;
  encourage the person to get help if needed.
- Let the person know you are thinking of her and
  praying for her; call or send a card in the mail once in
  a while, especially months after the event or on an
  anniversary.
- Don't assume that because a person seems happy and
  adjusted that the person is no longer grieving; be
  prepared for a wide range of feelings and reactions for
  a long time.
- Don't avoid the person; being there is more important
  than saying the right thing.

- Talk about the deceased person, tell stories, and keep the person alive through wonderful memories; it's important to know that a loved one is remembered.
- Don't judge; each person does the best she can.
- Laugh together.
- Pray for the person.

Helping Children Grieve

Children grieve differently from adults. Depending on their age and maturity, they may not understand the permanency of death and may have many questions about what happens next. A parent's death can affect a child's sense of security.

Grieving children may:

- revert to earlier behaviors, such as thumb sucking or bedwetting, or need extra help with simple tasks for their age, such as feeding or dressing themselves
- ask questions about details of the death or about the afterlife
- pretend it didn't happen
- talk with the deceased person at home, school, or in a place they view as a memorial
- change personality; become more aggressive or introverted; display mood swings
- test limits
- significantly increase or decrease risk-taking
- show physical signs of stress, such as nail biting, eye blinking, or other nervous habits
- become sick more often; complain of headaches, stomachaches, or general muscle aches
- feel angry about the way a loved one died; talk about getting revenge on bad guys or changing the world so people can't die that way anymore
- worry about other loved ones dying or leaving them

- fear being near the cause of death, such as fear of getting in a car after a loved one died in a car accident; worry that they will die of an illness or condition that their loved one died from, such as cancer or a heart attack; or fear that bad guys or natural disasters will harm their family
- talk about themselves dying too so they can be with the deceased person
- feel guilty or feel like they caused the person to die, especially if they ever wished it when they were angry
- lose interest in daily activities and events
- become easily distracted, have difficulty concentrating
- have trouble sleeping or eating
- fear being alone
- try to imitate or take over a role of the deceased loved one, for example, a young boy or teen might try to step into the role of a father
- experience loss of confidence or hope
- be confused about their identity (older children and teens especially) and how changes in their family due to this death may affect other aspects of their lives
- question their beliefs, such as how God answers prayers

When a Child Needs Help

Professional help may be needed if a child experiences a prolonged period of serious grief, such as continued loss of interest in activities, acting much younger for an extended time, repeated statements of wanting to join the deceased person, withdrawal from friends, excessive signs of stress, refusal to attend school, or a significant drop in school performance.

What you can do to help children grieve:

- Listen.
- Spend extra time with them.
- Talk honestly about the situation in terms they understand.
- Help them work through their feelings in creative ways, such as drawing pictures, writing in a journal, or writing poetry or music.
- Help them develop and maintain their sense of identity in this new situation.
- Explain changes before they experience them, such as a new neighborhood, school, church, or family routine.
- Keep tasks and responsibilities simple and manageable; help them take one step at a time.
- Keep routines as consistent and predictable as possible.
- Read stories about other children or characters who experience grief and sadness; this gives children a comfortable way to ask questions or open a discussion about how someone else felt and how they feel.
- Help them remember the person who died, especially any positive parts of the child's relationship with the person.
- Show them appropriate ways to cope and deal with their feelings.
- Encourage them to let you know when they are worried or having a difficult time.
- Provide lots of opportunities for play, fun, and laughter.

A Few Things I Have Learned

Much of grief is getting to the business of grieving. You may try to ignore it or walk around it, deny what has happened or convince yourself there was a good reason for it to happen. I certainly did until a friend of mine told me that the quickest way out of hell is to go straight through it. Don't try to go around, just straight through. That's not to say you can hurry grief or put it into a logical spreadsheet. (I tried this, too.) But to get past the worst of it, you have to face it head on. You have to acknowledge what has happened and the situation it leaves you in so you can sort through it. I am a widow. I am a single parent. It took me a long time to say that. I can't remember when I began to see the peace on the other side. But I do know that one day I woke up and knew it was my decision. I could stay in hell and struggle to breathe or I could choose to be happy, count my blessings, and accept the challenge to live God's plan rather than my own. A few things I have learned:

There are others who get it.

There are some things—summer camp, a military deployment, having your loved one die young—that you have to experience in order to truly understand. Although each person's story is unique, there is some small comfort when you find someone else in the room who understands just a bit about what there are no words to describe.

The Ultimate Deployment is much like the others.

A few weeks before my husband, Bob, died, I stood quietly at the edge of the bed, watching him sleep. I gently kissed his forehead and whispered, "I miss you so much." Dying of cancer, his body was failing the man I loved, the man who had come home safely from numerous deployments and two helicopter crashes. I could dole out pills and flush tubes, but how could I convince my Marine that this walker and wheel chair were mobility enablers? How could I help this man who had climbed mountains with me, who had fed starving children around the world and had stepped in harm's way to defend my freedoms, die gracefully and peacefully when it seemed our lives had just begun?

For some reason, in those final days, I thought constantly about our friends who were deployed. The emotion in our house was beginning to feel a lot like preparation for a deployment.

After a two-year battle with colon cancer, Bob left on what I call the Ultimate Deployment, on assignment in heaven.

Aside from the homecoming, I've found this deployment to be very similar to others. Things break, I'm a single parent, I wish I'd hear from him more, and I sometimes wonder how we'll make it through this one.

My life is like a novel.

It has helped me to think about my life as more than one book. The first book didn't end the way I thought it would, but it was still a really good book.

I've begun book two. I'm sort of in the prologue. There are some of the same characters in this new book, a few story lines continued, but there will be new ones, too. For a while I wanted to know all the answers—what the future would hold and what my role in it would be. But when I started thinking of my life as a book, I could say, just like with any good book, the enjoyment comes with reading each page, each chapter, seeing how the story unfolds—even with all its surprises—and maybe suggesting edits to God along the way.

People help each other.

Our son, Alexander, went head first into grief because he didn't know that denial was an option. Together we've learned some powerful life lessons that I hope will carry him through other challenges in his life.

One of these is that people help each other in tough times. He has seen our neighbors fix everything from our toilet to our roof. He understands what it means to have a friend who just listens or who cries with you.

Be kind to yourself.

Someone said that to me—"be kind to yourself"—and I didn't know what it meant. For me, I've learned it means a combination of forgiving myself for not being perfect and allowing myself to put my own needs first.

When Bob died, I lost my short-term memory. Fortunately, I'm around people with a sense of humor. I was also exhausted and had a joint injury that took a long time to heal. It seemed like Alexander and I were always getting sick and had a lot less patience with each other than we should have. I completely underestimated the physical toll grief can have.

I was overwhelmed by the thought of making any decision— big things like whether or not to stay in our house and little things like what to do with Bob's cologne. It took two years for me to find the energy to go through his clothes and donate them. When I did, there was a pair of jeans that still smelled like him.

After a while I accepted the fact that I might cry at any time, like when I hear a certain song or do really emotional things like buy printer toner at Office Max.

The hardest part for me has been making quiet time for myself, time to reflect, to rest and feed my spirit. It took a while to have the courage to listen to what I might say to myself if I actually slowed down and reflected. I'm finally past most of the nightmares and now I do put at the top of my list to eat healthy foods and exercise. I'm still working on sleep.

You can celebrate the person who died and still move on to celebrate your own life today.

We send up balloons on Father's Day and Bob's birthdays (birth on Earth and into heaven). Alexander loves to watch our wedding reception video. It was a great party and a great example of Bob at his happiest. There's a poster hanging in Alexander's room with a collage of photos of his dad and once in a while he asks to hear a story about one of them.

Yet we are our own family, too. We're a team—the two of us. We are making our own traditions and celebrations and good memories.

Take one step at a time.

There is something freeing about recognizing your reality and then dealing with it. Whether that's finances or learning how to cook (Bob was our cook, but Alexander says I make the best jelly sandwiches and hot dogs) or figuring out who you really are in your new life, what things you like to do and who you want to be now that everything's changed in what you thought was the plan.

To deal with it and make it less overwhelming, I take one step. Just one. And then the next usually comes.

There is no time limit to grief.

People around you who don't know this may create time expectations about wedding rings, belongings, and moving on. You'll know you are ready when you are ready. And you can change your mind. I took off my wedding ring one year after Bob died. Three days later I put it back on and wore it for more than another year. Some days I wear it now to feel close to Bob. We each make our own decisions.

We adapt. It is amazing what we will get used to, forget, or apply reasoning to in order to manage pain and guilt so we can function in daily life. Over time, nightmares do give way to loving memories. Alexander told me that God lets us forget the bad stuff so we can remember the good memories and feel joy. I learn a lot from Alexander.

And so time (and love, tears, and laughter) does heal some wounds. But even years later, there may be moments—certain decisions, reminders, milestones—in which you long for the person with all your heart and the most reasonable thing to do is sit on the floor and cry because he really isn't coming back.

Grace may come in unexpected ways.

I've been a writer all my life, but when Bob died, I had no words. For months, I couldn't write, not even in a journal. Then one night when I was standing at the stove trying to cook something other than hot dogs for dinner, I started to sing. Since that night, I've written about thirty songs. They express what it's like to move through this experience. Bob was a music lover. I believe this was a gift from him to help me get those feelings out, to find my words again.

God is a weaver.

God takes all the scraps, all the colors of our life, and just keeps weaving them. We can't see the whole tapestry and how it will all come together, but each piece is important and celebrates a wonderful blessing from our life.

This deployment is the most difficult. But it's also Bob's most important mission ever.

I don't understand why things have happened this way. But every now and then I see a glimpse of how my experience helps someone else and that's when I'm reminded that in God's plan, I'm right where I'm supposed to be.

~

Whether you are working through challenges of an injury, the death of a loved one, or grieving a different loss, know that your experience is part of something bigger than any of us can imagine. Have faith that you will soon find joy and laughter again. Enjoy the little blessings in your day, such as a sunset, a special moment with a loved one, a kind word from a friend. They are kisses on the cheek from heaven to let you know you are loved and just where you ought to be.

Chapter Five

Continuing the Journey

Months into your reunion, you may find it is taking longer than you anticipated to get in the swing of your new normal. You and your service member may have different expectations about how long it takes to get back into an integrated routine with daily responsibilities. Longer term decisions about careers or lifestyles may have surfaced after a few months of reflecting on the experience. It may take longer than you expect to rebuild trust and intimacy. You may have had serious events happen during the deployment that you are still working through. Or you may find yourself preparing for another deployment while you are trying to reunite from this one.

Kara Kitchen-Glodgett (wife):
I was resentful after a couple months of him being home. I thought, "When can I relax and take a break? Demand more from him? He's the hero, but what about me?" He wasn't on a vacation, but neither was I. When I finally asked for his help, he needed to hear it as much as I needed to say it. We weren't in competition with each other and it was challenging for both of us. Talking it through strengthened our bond even more.

Amy Palecek (wife):
My husband says I still don't include him in a lot of things. He wants to be included, but does not know how to say it without seeming to butt in on my routine. I want him to help, but do not know if he will think I am forcing him

into our life. It is so easy to take for granted that he is home, his presence is felt. I want so badly to not let the everyday routine take away from it, but the routine is sometimes the challenge. All day long I think of things I want to tell him, and then when we are together, the baby has a need or the three year old is telling a story, then bath and bed time, and before I know it a day has passed.

Deanna Wellsted (wife):

My husband, Scott, said he had a lot of time to think. He had spent twelve years in the Marines and was in the first Gulf War. He spent nine years as a civilian federal police officer and then went back to Iraq with the Army National Guard. He decided to go to law school with a minor in business so he could focus on more of the administrative side of law versus the constant life threatening.

Boyce Folliot (soldier):

Before I was diagnosed with PTSD, I didn't understand why I couldn't be with my wife. I knew deep down I still loved her. But I had a really hard time. I couldn't talk with her about it. I wasn't sure what I was feeling. I know it really hurt Amelie. I still have a hard time describing it. Those months are like a fog to me. My mind was somewhere else.

Some military families find they are still working on adjustments a year after a long deployment. Close relationships are hard work under any circumstances, certainly under the strain you experienced through this deployment and reunion. Keep the faith. Talk with your chaplain and others who have been through this so you have support as you continue to rebuild relationships with your loved ones.

Much of Life is Perspective

The time you were separated from your loved one in this deployment can seem like a long time. Within that span of time babies learn to walk, teenagers go to college, and friendships, jobs, and water heaters may all come and go.

But no matter how long this deployment was and no matter what your relationship is to the person deployed, this deployment was a very short time compared to spending your life together. You might compare it to a pregnancy, the toddler years of your life, one job out of a career. It is one experience. An important one, but still just one aspect.

Keep in mind this perspective as you rebuild your relationships and continue the journey to the next chapter of your life.

This deployment is a very short time

compared to spending your life together.

A Day for a Day

Lana Schmidtke shares, "We went through a lot of changes over the 411 days Dan was deployed, and we realized that not only was the world not built in a day but neither was our relationship. Going slow and adjusting to the new us after those 411 days is something we continue to build on each day."

Chaplain Imhoff encourages, "Be patient with your family. 'A day for a day.' Allow one day of reintegration for each day of deployment. It takes time."

Rebuilding with Your Spouse

Barb and Jerry Kraft grew as a couple in this experience. "You express things in love letters, why you love each other," Barb says. "We had allowed other obligations to take over before but now we make time to focus on each other and our love. When we get strong tempered, we just look at each other and ask 'Is it worth fighting over?' Our time together is valuable."

Lana and Dan Schmidtke also grew closer. "We talked about things we never would have had he been here," Lana said. "Our favorite color, stupid little things, in a dating process." Lana and Dan also realized they need positive support outside their relationship. "Even with a great relationship," says Lana, "we have to be able to vent and talk outside the marriage or we would have thrown in the towel shortly after he came home. We've both changed a lot and it's been hard not knowing for sure how the other would take what we needed to say. We continue to take one day at a time knowing that each day is bringing us one step closer to understanding what we need to do to survive the next round of deployment and reunion."

Chaplain Steven Lambert shared one of his favorite sayings with me. He said, "Love begins when you expect nothing in return." Deacon Rip Riordan added, "True love is the will to do good for others at cost to self."

And that's the thing about marriage. It's not what you get— it's what you give. Marriage is not about equality. It's not about what the other person does for you. It's about how you show your love, ways you honor your partner and friend all the days of your life. Any time you start to feel like you aren't getting your fair share, instead think about what else you can do to show your love.

Creating Trust with Children

Barb Kraft (wife):

When his classmate's dad deployed to Bosnia, our eight-year-old son, Jared, prayed for her family every night. "I'm the only one who knows how Alicia feels," he said.

Our ten-year-old, Caleb, was angry with his dad. He felt his dad had a choice and left him. They needed to work it out. Slowly, his anger has gone away. He doesn't talk about it much.

Jean Denney (fiancée):

The three-year-old twins carried their dad's picture around and looked for him everywhere after he left again from his two weeks of R&R leave. They had a hard time trusting him when he got home. They thought he would leave again. He dropped off and picked up the kids each day to Grandma's and school to earn back their trust.

If you are still having difficulty at this point in the reunion rebuilding relationships with your children, the issue is likely trust. Young children want to trust you and love you. But most are also very tangible, black and white thinkers. Make a conscious effort to earn back their trust and confidence.

"Having a toddler try to trust someone he doesn't know is a challenge," says Barb Kraft. "Isaac was fifteen months old when his dad came back. Now he's almost three and they still have trust issues."

Children may also still have difficulty understanding what really happened during the separation. For middle-grade children, you may need to reassure them the separation was not their fault and that it was necessary for their parent to help other people in the world, too. Help them feel a larger connection to the world by sharing information about the people and culture where their parent was deployed. Let them empathize and help others. When we share our experience or use the wisdom we've gained or simply are there for someone else just because we understand, it helps us feel that our experience had a purpose and in some ways helps us better understand our own experience.

Connecting with Teens

Adam Mitchell (soldier):

I had gained custody of my teenage daughter right before my deployment to Bosnia. A few months into the deployment, she started giving me subtle hints she wanted to move back with her mother. Our conversations became more heated until she was demanding it. I was against it because it wasn't a good environment for her to be in.

When Cynthia had lived with her mom, she had become clinically depressed, with suicidal tendencies. She cut herself. It was not a good place for her to move back to. I have a psych background (one of the main reasons the judge awarded me custody—my ex-wife was not at all equipped to deal with this). Once I was out of the picture, deployed, my ex-wife started saying things to Cynthia like "It must be really hard, wouldn't it be better if you moved back?" My ex-wife could have been supportive, but she saw a chance to regain custody. This fueled Cynthia's depression.

By the time I got home, Cynthia and I had an extremely difficult, strained relationship. You hope for a nice healthy, fun reunion but it was completely filled with stress and anxiety. My ex-wife had been working on her to get her to come back to Nevada, where she grew up. But she didn't tell Cynthia she planned to sell the Nevada home and move to Philadelphia. The attraction for Cynthia was to be with her childhood friends in Nevada; her mother lied to her.

Cynthia is doing fabulously now. How did they work it out? "Honesty and open communication," Adam says. "We look at lessons learned—when there are hidden agendas, when people are motivated by non-honorable reasons, it can be hurtful. If we want to live worthwhile, proud, honorable lives, we don't condone that behavior." They have used this experience as a lesson learned. "It was hard, stressful, tearful, difficult. But now we take it and use it to our benefit." He has frank conversations with her. "We enjoy a good, open relationship," he says. "She tells me stuff that some-times I think I don't want to hear. About girls and what they are doing with sex or drugs. I feel good that she feels secure to bring these issues to me."

Teens are on that bridge between child and adult, the land of proms, pimples, and self-expression. They don't have the expe-rience to make adult decisions yet don't want you making their decisions for them either. Help your teen learn positive coping skills for stressful situations such as school demands, negative thoughts about themselves or their appearance, changes in their bodies, problems with friends. Be interested and attentive and hear what they have to say. Take an interest in their friends. Talk to them about risks. Give them space to express themselves, but be available whenever they need you. Be a role model they want to follow. And keep the door open.

Exploring New Relationships Between Parents and Service Members

Deanna Wellsted (mom):

Your child leaves home a child, comes back a man. It's a life-altering experience. Chad (age twenty-two) came home from Iraq before his dad who was also deployed there. He had a hard time dealing with the rules of the house. He said, "You can't tell me what to do. I've been doing this and survived." Within a couple months, he moved out to start college thirty minutes away. I don't see him much but I know he's having a hard time adjusting and I don't know what to do.

Julie LaBelle (mom):

My son was the peanut I raised. With my whole heart, my life's goal was to protect and nurture him. Even the concept of having his own rifle rattled me. One of my challenges has been to treat him as the man he is now and to let go! A tall order for a mom under any circumstances.

Sometimes the hardest part of being a parent is letting go of your view of your son or daughter as a child and seeing that child as an adult. You know your loved ones better than anyone. Take your cues from them. Do they need you to back off? Or do they need more of your support? Follow your instincts.

Coping with News of a Pending Deployment or Feelings About Going Back

Chaplain Imhoff notes that a major challenge for many military families is being reunited only to be told that the unit will be deploying again in nine to thirteen months. "Families have not had time to experience the reunion/reintegration process when they are thrown into the deployment preparation phase. I have had comments made to me like: 'We do not know which phase of the deployment cycle we are in.' The truth is that military families are living in deployment preparation and reunion/reintegration at the same time. So they are trying to adjust after deployment at the same time they are preparing for another separation. This can play havoc with emotions. There is a switch that many people turn on and off at times of deployment. To avoid emotional hurt, they try to cover their emotions. Knowing that they will be separated, they try to disconnect as the day of separation nears. Then, during mid-tour leave, they are excited about seeing their loved ones, but at the same time they know that they will be separated in two weeks. Then comes redeployment. The emotions gear up around the excitement of being reunited. Then following the homecoming, they are told they will be separated again. It is like being on an emotional roller coaster that can create a wall between husbands and wives, parents and children. Families hope for more time between deployments, but can be separated two years of a three-year tour at an installation. This puts a greater strain on families, because the deployment announcement often comes at a time of joy (reunion)."

Barb Kraft (wife):

The six-month mark was the hardest for us. Jerry felt the job in Iraq was undone and he needed to go back there. He missed the people he served with and bonded with. It was really hard for me to hear that he wanted to be back there.

Katherine Leland (wife):

Jacob is still in the Guard and continues to drill once every month, but every time he leaves to go to drill I feel like he is being deployed all over again.

June Mickleby (mom):

My son has only been back in the States six months. He already has orders to deploy again. How can he possibly be ready to do that? He had surgery on his shoulder and it isn't healed yet. I'm not ready yet. I want to send them a note that says he does not have his mother's permission!

Lana Schmidtke (wife):

I have to say the hardest part of reunion for us has been the all too frequent notifications of deployment and return for many of our colleagues and friends. With each new notification that someone is going to be traveling the same journey that we have traveled we all tend to go back in time thinking of our struggles and the milestones we have passed. In a sense each activation we hear about takes us back in time.

Some families decide the way to deal with the rollercoaster is to end the ride.

Stacy Westbrook (wife):

My husband deployed to Macedonia, Germany, Kosovo, Kuwait, and then Iraq. Our seven-year-old son met his dad when he was five months old, then his dad left at nine

months old for seven months to Kosovo. He has been
through five of his dad's deployments in his seven years of
life. He doesn't take it well. Our five-year-old daughter has
been through three deployments. Iraq was the hardest. She
broke her leg and cried for her dad. It's a tough life. We are
done. (Seven months after his return from Iraq, Stacy's
husband left the Army.)

Others realize this really is the life they are meant to live,
despite the ups and downs.

Shannon Roberts (wife):
    His enlistment was up at the time of his return and he
elected to get out. That lasted a whole three months and he
reenlisted, this time with a local National Guard unit. He
realized how much he missed it and that it is truly in his
blood. He sometimes talks about maybe doing another
rotation, but then thinks about the opposite side and doesn't
really pursue it. I just tell him that whatever he decides to do,
we are behind him 100%.

Heather Greene Hinckley (wife):
    Howard is very much a soldier. He is ready and willing to
go back to the Middle East because he feels he is still needed
there and that the mission is not complete.

Those families for whom the military remains a career or
lifestyle choice offer a few ways to cope with the rollercoaster:

- Focus on today, not what may or may not come
  tomorrow.
- Enjoy each moment you have together.
- Don't sweat the small stuff.
- Get and keep a good Mother Hen.
- Every day do something special that shows how much
  you love each other.
- Say "I love you."

- Hug, hold hands, smile.
- Keep the faith.

The Next Chapter in the Journey

Your reunion experience is different from anyone else's, including your own previous reunions. Each time you go through this, your age, maturity, experience, the mission situation, and support are all different. Yet you've likely found some similarities between your experience and the experiences of other military families in this book. Perhaps you have experienced:

- a fairytale homecoming…
  or a disappointing homecoming
- an enriching reunion, bringing your family even closer together and helping you appreciate each day
- adjustments getting used to living in the same house again, figuring out new routines, establishing new communication
- rebuilding relationships, perhaps that need extra attention even after several months together
- continued worry about your family's safety and health
- long-term decisions, such as career changes or lifestyle choices
- dealing with the effects of anxiety, stress, or depression
- figuring out how to live without a friend or loved one who died

There are many military family reunions that have a happy ending. And also many that go through serious challenges along the journey. You may be tempted to hurry through it. But we can't skip to the end of our book. We need to live each page as our story unfolds, even with its turns and surprises and rollercoaster rides.

Reread "The Answers" at the beginning of this book. Laugh good hearty belly laughs every day. See through the eyes of love with every word you speak or action you take. Buy more underwear so you can do less of the mundane and more of what's important to you.

This is your chance to begin the next chapter of your journey. Make it a wonderful adventure!

Appendix

Resources for Your Happily Ever After

Happily Ever After. Isn't that how books are supposed to end? We all know that Cinderella doesn't have the only version of a happy ending.

Write your own version of happily ever after. And use these resources, recommended by other military families, to help you with the bumps on the journey.

Please check www.lifeafterdeployment.com for an updated list with links and to recommend resources you have found helpful.

Deployment and Reunion

Surviving Deployment: A guide for military families
by Karen M. Pavlicin
Personal stories and practical ideas to guide you through all aspects of deployment.

A Year of Absence: Six women's stories of courage, hope, and love
by Jessica Redmond
Follows six women during their husbands' deployment to Iraq as part of the Army's First Armored Division based in Baumholder, Germany.

Deployment Journal for Kids
by Rachel Robertson
A special place for kids to express feelings and record events during a loved one's deployment. Contains calendar pages, writing ideas, interesting facts about common deployment locations, military definitions, and a pocket to keep mementos.

Love, Lizzie: Letters to a military mom
by Lisa Tucker McElroy
Nine-year-old Lizzie writes to her mother, who is deployed overseas during wartime, and includes maps that show her mother what Lizzie has been thinking and doing. Includes tips for helping children of military families.

Daddy, You're My Hero! and **Mommy, You're My Hero!**
by Michelle Ferguson-Cohen
The same story is offered in two different versions for children with a dad or a mom in the military. Helps young children feel good about their parent's job "to make people safe... and a good world for me."

Night Catch
by Brenda Ehrmantraut
When a soldier's work takes him half-way around the world, he enlists the help of the North Star for a nightly game of catch with his son.

When Dad's at Sea
by Mindy Pelton
Emily's dad leaves for a six-month deployment. The story tells how Emily copes and counts time until his return; she tears off a piece of paper chain each day and traces his journey on a map.

Courage After Fire: Coping strategies for returning soldiers and their families
by Keith Armstrong, LCSW, Suzanne Best, PhD, and
Paula Domenici, PhD
Guide for veterans of OIF and OEF. Includes common reactions that can occur after serving in a war zone and specific strategies to address them. Topics include PTSD, grief, depression, drug abuse, and changes in your view of the world and yourself.

Down Range: To Iraq and back
by Bridget C. Cantrell, PhD and Chuck Dean
Guide for returning troops and their families. Topics include flashbacks, depression, fits of rage, nightmares, anxiety, emotional numbing, and other troubling aspects of PTSD.

Getting Home: All the way home (DVD)
Discusses basic post-deployment readjustment concerns and offers encouragement for returning service members.
www.ptsdresources.org

SurvivingDeployment.com
Information, articles, and resources about deployment.
www.survivingdeployment.com

DeploymentKids.com
Noncommercial, fun site for military kids. Downloadable cards and hero certificates, information about deployment locations, ideas for kids.
www.deploymentkids.com

Department of Defense Deployment Health and Family Readiness Library
Information about deployment and reunion for service members, families, and health care providers.
deploymenthealthlibrary.fhp.osd.mil

DeploymentLINK
A DoD site with links to family resources in each service.
deploymentlink.osd.mil/deploy/family/family_support.shtml

Operation Child Care
Program designed to support the short-term child care needs of National Guard and Reserve members in OIF or OEF. Child care providers from across the country donate a minimum of four hours of child care for service members home for R&R.
www.childcareaware.org/en/operationchildcare

Marine Corps Community Services
Deployment & reunion information.
www.usmc-mccs.org/deploy

Department of Veterans Affairs Medical Centers
The VA's main site for veterans returning from Iraq and Afghanistan. Lists local VA offices and hospitals. Also includes information on benefits and transition assistance.
www.seamlesstransition.va.gov

U.S. Dept. of Veterans Affairs Readjustment Counseling Service
Offers a range of services to combat veterans and their families, including individual counseling, group counseling, marital and family counseling, bereavement counseling, medical referrals, assistance in applying for VA benefits, employment counseling, alcohol/drug assessments, information and referral to community resources, military sexual trauma counseling and referral, outreach, and community education.
www.va.gov/rcs
800-827-1000 or 202-273-9116

Military Family Centers and Support Groups

Your local chaplain
To find your local chaplain's number, look in your base directory or look up your unit on the Internet and search the online directory for the chaplain's office.

Your local family readiness group/family support group
You should receive a key contact or volunteer leader name from your service member's unit. You may also contact the headquarters family center program for your branch and ask for the closest family center.

Air Force Family Support Center
www.affsc.org

Army Community and Family Support Center
www.armymwr.com
Army Family Assistance Hotline: 800-833-6622
Army Reserve Hotline: 800-318-5298

Marine Corps Community Service Centers
www.usmc-mccs.org
West of Mississippi: 800-253-1624
East of Mississippi: 800-336-4663

Navy Fleet and Family Service Center
www.nffsp.org
Naval Services Family Line: 877-673-7773

Army Reserve Family Programs
Provides information on family program support offices, Reserve family member benefits, family readiness handbooks, and Reserve family news.
www.arfp.org

National Guard Family Program
Programs, benefits, resources, family readiness for Guard families.
www.guardfamily.org

Morale, Welfare, and Recreation
www.armymwr.com
www.mwr.navy.mil

FRG Forum
An online community for and about Family Readiness Group leadership.
FRG.army.mil

vFRG
Sign up to join your unit's vFRG or learn how your FRG can go virtual.
www.armyfrg.org

General Military Life

Military HOMEFRONT
Official DoD quality of life Web site designed to assist service members and their families as well as commanders and service providers with a wide range of information on military life. Includes a directory of all military installations with phone numbers and Web sites for family and childcare centers.
www.militaryhomefront.dod.mil

Military OneSource
Trained counselors provide information over the help line and make referrals. You may receive free counseling in your community—up to six sessions per issue, paid for by DoD. The counseling focuses on stress management and relationship issues. It is not the medical health care required for depression, PTSD, or other serious conditions. All members of the Army, Air Force, Marine Corps, and Navy active duty, National Guard, Reserve, and their families are eligible for this 24x7 service.

www.militaryonesource.com
800-342-9647
You can also reach the program by telephone or through the Web site for your service branch:

- Army OneSource at 800-464-8107 or www.armyonesource.com
- Air Force OneSource at 800-707-5784 or www.airforceonesource.com
- MCCS OneSource at 800-869-0278 or www.mccsonesource.com
- Navy OneSource at 800-540-4123 or www.navyonesource.com

You can register with an id/password and view articles on the sites.

Air Force Crossroads
Official community Web site of the Air Force. Provides information on Air Force installations, family separation and readiness, benefits, and relocation.
www.afcrossroads.com

Army Family Team Building
A volunteer-led organization that provides training and information to Army family members.
www.armyfamilyteambuilding.org

Army Families Online
Information, articles, and resources about Army life.
www.armyfamiliesonline.org

My Army Life
A Web site for learning about Army family life.
www.myarmylifetoo.com

Marine Corps Family Network
Web site dedicated to providing support for Marine Corps families.
www.marinefamily.com

Navy LIFELines
Provides online resources in areas such as deployment readiness, family support, transition assistance, and MWR.
www.lifelines.navy.mil

Military.com
Information and commentary on pay and benefits, careers, education, transition assistance, current events, and more.
www.military.com

Military Spouse Magazine
A bimonthly magazine written by, for, and about US military spouses, with content that addresses all aspects of military life.
www.militaryspousemagazine.com

BooksForBrats.net
Home of the books *Daddy, You're My Hero!* and *Mommy, You're My Hero!* Also includes downloadable stickers and certificates, and ecards.
www.booksforbrats.net

Blue Star Moms
Nonprofit association for mothers who now have, or have had, children serving in the military.
www.bluestarmothers.org

*Cin*CHouse
Online magazine and Web-based community for military wives, girlfriends, and women in uniform.
www.cinchouse.com

MilitaryFamilyBooks.com
Online store with books and music about military life.
www.militaryfamilybooks.com

Military Spouse Blog
A virtual family support group. Authors and site visitors contribute to the blog on all aspects of military life. Current news links keep you up on what's going on in the military community at large.
www.spousebuzz.com

Marine Parents
Support for mothers, fathers, spouses, family and friends of Marines.
www.marine-parents.com

Sarah Smiley's Misadventures
Stories from a syndicated columnist, author, and military wife.
www.sarahsmiley.com

Associations and Support Services

Association of the United States Army (AUSA)
Private, nonprofit educational organization that supports Army service members, retirees, and family members.
www.ausa.org
800-336-4570

Military Child Education Coalition
Nonprofit organization that identifies the challenges that military children face and works with military and educational communities to implement programs to meet the challenges.
www.militarychild.org
254-953-1923

National Military Family Association
Nonprofit organization that serves military families and survivors through education, information, and advocacy. Promotes and protects the interests of military families by influencing the development and implementation of legislation and policies affecting them.
www.nmfa.org
800-260-0218

TRICARE
The worldwide health care program for uniformed service members, active duty and retired, and their families.
www.tricare.osd.mil
800-DOD-Cares

TRICARE Reserve Select
Health insurance for eligible National Guard and Reserve members.
www.tricare.osd.mil/reserve/reserveselect

USAA
Provides products and services, such as auto and home insurance, investment services, and financial planning to help military members and their families reach their financial goals.
www.usaa.com

USO
Nonprofit organization that provides morale, welfare, and recreation-type services to service members and families.
www.uso.org

The U.S. Department of Veterans Affairs
Government agency responsible for administering veterans benefits for veterans, their families, and survivors.
www.va.gov
800-827-1000

Veterans Benefits Administration
Information about compensation, pension, home loans, and more.
www.vba.va.gov
800-827-1000

Service Branches

Air Force
www.af.mil

Army
www.army.mil

Coast Guard
www.uscg.mil

Marines
www.usmc.mil

Navy
www.navy.mil

Air National Guard
www.ang.af.mil

Army National Guard
www.arng.army.mil

National Guard Bureau
www.ngb.army.mil

Air Force Reserve Command
www.afrc.af.mil

Army Reserve
www.armyreserve.army.mil

Coast Guard Reserve
www.uscg.mil/reserve

Marine Forces Reserve
www.mfr.usmc.mil

Navy Reserve
www.navyreserve.navy.mil

Military Services Relief Societies

Air Force Aid Society
www.afas.org
800-769-8951

Army Emergency Relief
www.aerhq.org
866-878-6378 or 703-428-0000

Coast Guard Mutual Assistance
www.cgmahq.org
800-881-2462

Navy-Marine Corps Relief Society
www.nmcrs.org
703-696-4904

American Red Cross
www.redcross.org
202-303-4498

Parenting

Parenting with Love and Logic
by Foster W. Cline and Jim Fay
The authors advocate raising responsible children by helping them learn how to make choices and learn from the consequences. Includes strategies for applying this parenting method to actual situations, such as back-seat battles in the car, homework, and keeping bedrooms clean.

Queen Bees and Wannabes: Helping your daughter survive cliques, gossip, boyfriends, and other realities of adolescence
by Rosalind Wiseman
Helps parents understand their daughters' friendships, the power of cliques, and the roles within them. Discusses boys, drugs, and sex. Author outlines parenting styles and offers tips for talking to teens.

Raising Cain: Protecting the emotional life of boys
by Dan Kindlon and Michael Thompson
Identifies the social and emotional challenges that boys encounter in school and shows how parents can help boys cultivate emotional awareness and empathy, giving them the connections and support they need to navigate the social pressures of youth.

Why Do They Act That Way?: A survival guide to the adolescent brain for you and your teen
by David Walsh, PhD
Explains what happens to the brain on the path from childhood into adolescence and adulthood. Shows why moodiness, quickness to anger and to take risks, and other familiar teenage behaviors are so common.

Babycenter.com
Comprehensive parenting site with a community board and articles organized by topic, including getting pregnant, pregnancy, baby, toddler, preschooler, and big kid.
www.babycenter.com

American Academy of Pediatrics
Pediatricians offer information on a variety of health and development topics for infants, children, and adolescents.
www.aap.org/topics.html

KidsHealth
Sponsored by Nemours Foundation. Health topics are organized into three sites: for parents, for children, and for teens.
www.kidshealth.org

Anger, Depression, Stress, and PTSD

The Anger Control Workbook
by Matthew McKay and Peter Rogers
Step-by-step exercises to help identify, understand, respond to, and cope with anger.

The Depression Workbook: A guide for living with depression and manic depression, second edition
by Mary Ellen Copeland and Matthew McKay
Overview of symptoms and treatments, with space for you to write your own thoughts about treatment, prognosis, and your ultimate goals. Checklists and daily planners. Charts for tracking medications, diet, and doctor visits.

All About Depression
Information about causes, symptoms, treatment, and medications for depression.
www.allaboutdepression.com

Depression and Bipolar Support Alliance
Patient-directed nonprofit organization that provides information about depression and bipolar disorder and organizes support groups across the country.
www.dbsalliance.org
800-826-3632

Vietnam Wives: Facing the challenges of life with veterans suffering post-traumatic stress
by Aphrodite Matsakis, PhD
A look at how to recognize and manage combat stress and how it affects everyone in the family. Includes stories of women whose husbands served in Vietnam.

Finding My Way: A teen's guide to living with a parent who has experienced trauma
by Michelle D. Sherman, Ph.D. and DeAnne M. Sherman
Explains PTSD and other common responses to trauma as well as treatment options. Encourages readers to address their own emotions including anger, fear, confusion, sadness, and shame. Includes coping tools, frequently asked questions, a glossary, and resource list.

Straight Talk About Post-Traumatic Stress Disorder: Coping with the aftermath of trauma
by Kay Marie Porterfield
Includes an overview of PTSD from several different causes, plus symptoms, treatment, the process of recovery, and sources of help.

Coping with Post-Traumatic Stress Disorder
by Carolyn Simpson and Dwain Simpson
Discusses situations such as physical abuse, natural disasters, wars, and violence that can cause stressful responses and describes ways of dealing with these delayed reactions to trauma.

The PTSD Workbook: Simple, effective techniques for overcoming traumatic stress symptoms
by Mary Beth Williams and Soili Poijula
Techniques and interventions to conquer trauma-related symptoms.

National Center for Post-Traumatic Stress Disorder
A special center within Veterans Affairs that supports veterans through research, education, and training in the science, diagnosis, and treatment of PTSD and stress-related conditions.
www.ncptsd.org
802-296-6300

International Society for Traumatic Stress Studies (ISTSS)
Information about trauma, loss, and traumatic grief.
www.istss.org
847-480-9028

PTSDSupport.net
Informative PTSD site written and maintained by a wounded Vietnam-era veteran. Includes symptoms, treatment, and resources for PTSD, combat stress, compassion fatigue, and more.
www.ptsdsupport.net

PTSDResources.org
Sponsored by Military Chaplains Associated Services. Includes articles by Dr. Michael Colson, a two-tour Iraq/Afghan Vet.
www.ptsdresources.org

Living with Injuries

Military Severely Injured Center
Support for severely injured veterans, including a job search database, listing of veteran-friendly employers, and information about career events, resumes, and salaries.
888-774-1361

Operation Warfighter
Sponsorted by Military Severely Injured Center. Temporary assignment program for service members who are undergoing therapy at military treatment facilities in the United States. Designed to provide meaningful activity outside of the hospital environment and offer a formal means of transition back to the military or civilian workforce.
www.militaryhomefront.dod.mil/operationwarfighter

Air Force Palace HART (Helping Airmen Recover Together)
Follows Air Force wounded until they return to active duty or medically retire. Provides information and counseling on military benefits.
Contact through Military Severely Injured Center, 888-774-1361

U.S. Army Wounded Warrior Program (AW2)
Assists soldiers with severe disabilities and their families in their transition from military service and into the civilian community. Web site includes links, FAQs, resource information and counselors by region.
www.aw2.army.mil
800-237-1336

Marine for Life

Supports wounded Marines and their families from the time of injury through return to service. Provides transition assistance to Marines who honorably leave active service and return to civilian life. Web site lists local contacts by state and provides information on benefits, assistive technologies, forms, and more.
www.m4l.usmc.mil
866-645-8762 or 703-784-9140

Navy Safe Harbor

Provides support and assistance to sailors who suffer from severe injuries incurred in support of the Global War on Terrorism. Encourages active duty retention and provides continuing support for sailors with 30% or more disability rating transitioning to civilian life.
www.npc.navy.mil/CommandSupport/SafeHarbor
877-746-8563

Always a Soldier

Provides veterans with service-connected disabilities the opportunity to seek employment and career advancement. The program is an Army Material Command initiative, and the Web site provides information regarding the program, employment opportunities, and links.
www.amc.army.mil/alwaysasoldier
703-806-8140

Blinded Veterans Association

Helps veterans and their families meet the challenges of blindness and promotes the welfare of blinded veterans.
www.bva.org
202-371-8880

CAUSE: Comfort for America's Uniformed Services Elite

Provides comfort items for troops recuperating in military hospitals and rehabilitation centers from wounds and injuries.
www.cause-usa.org
703-481-8830

Coalition to Salute America's Heroes
Homes for Wounded War Heroes Fund brings together community partners to renovate homes for wheelchair-bound and blind veterans.
www.saluteheroes.org
914-432-5400

Defense and Veterans Brain Injury Center
Serves active duty military, their dependents and veterans with traumatic brain injury (TBI) through medical care, clinical research initiatives, and educational programs.
www.dvbic.org
800-870-9244 or 202-782-6345

Disabled Transition Assistance Program (DTAP)
The Transition Assistance Program (TAP) was established to meet the needs of separating service members during their period of transition into civilian life by offering job-search assistance and related services. Service members leaving the military with a service-connected disability are offered DTAP. Includes the normal three-day TAP workshop, plus additional hours of individual instruction to help determine job readiness and address the special needs of veterans with disabilities.
www.dol.gov/vets/programs/tap/main.htm
866-4-USA-DOL (866-487-2365)

DoD Vets
Provides a wide range of information relating to DoD employment opportunities for veterans with disabilities.
www.dodvets.com

Fisher House Foundation
Donates comfort homes, built on the grounds of major military and VA medical centers. These homes enable family members to be close to a loved one during hospitalization for an unexpected illness, disease, or injury. The average charge is less than $10 per family per day, with many locations offering rooms at no cost.
www.fisherhouse.org
888-294-8560 or 301-294-8560

Global War on Terrorism Veterans in Need
Provides support programs for returning disabled service members.
www.gwtvetsinneed.org

Homes for Our Troops
Assists injured veterans and their families by building new or adapting existing homes for handicapped accessibility.
www.homesforourtroops.org
866-7-TROOPS (866-787-6677)

National Amputation Foundation
Offers peer counseling and referrals to veterans who are amputees.
www.nationalamputation.org
516-887-3600

Operation First Response
Supports wounded veterans and their families.
www.operationfirstresponse.org

Death and Grief

Tragedy Assistance Program for Survivors, Inc. (TAPS)
Peer support network for surviving family members of deceased service members. Holds annual National Military Survivor Seminar and Good Grief Camp for Young Survivors over Memorial Day weekend.
www.taps.org
800-959-TAPS (800-959-8277)
202-588-TAPS (202-588-8277)

Society of Military Widows
Offers support for widows of deceased service members.
www.militarywidows.org
800-842-3451

Gold Star Wives
Organization of military widows and widowers whose spouse died while on active duty or from service connected disabilities.
www.goldstarwives.org
888-751-6350

American Gold Star Mothers
Organization of mothers whose son or daughter died in service to our country.
www.goldstarmoms.com
202-265-0991

Air Force Survivor Assistance
Assists surviving family members of deceased Air Force personnel with benefits, information, and support.
survivorassistance.afsv.af.mil
877-USAFHELP (877-872-3435)

Army Families First Casualty Call Center (FFCCC)
Assists surviving family members of deceased Army soldiers with questions about benefits, outreach, advocacy, and support.
www.ArmyFamiliesFirst.army.mil
866-272-5841

Military Relief Societies
Contact your service branch relief society for lifetime benefits information to the surviving spouse (or child if there is no spouse). Provided on behalf of the society by the Armed Forces Service Corporation (AFSC). ASFC also helps with claim processing, survivor benefits, and family assistance needs.
See **Military Services Relief Societies** earlier in this appendix.

Special Operations Warrior Foundation
Provides college scholarship grants, financial aid, and educational counseling to children of special operations personnel killed in action.
www.specialops.org
877-337-7693 or 813-805-9400

United Warrior Survivor Foundation (UWSF)
Offers programs and services to surviving spouses of special operations personnel who have been killed in the line of duty since 9-11-2001.
www.FrogFriends.com
877-804-UWSF (877-804-8973)

The U.S. Department of Veterans Affairs

Offers bereavement counseling to parents, spouses, and children of Armed Forces members who died in service. You'll also find information and applications for compensation, health, burial, special programs, and other benefits on the Web site.

www.va.gov

202-273-9116

Fallen Heroes Memorial

A site where you can list information about the person who died and invite friends and family to post messages.

www.fallenheroesmemorial.com

Young Widows

An online support group for young widows and widowers. Provides a listing of local support groups, book recommendations, and links to online discussion groups and Web sites.

www.youngwidow.org

Young Widows or Widowers (YWOW)

Offers bereavement resources, workshops, forums, meetings, and social events to help young widows and widowers "rebuild our lives, dreams, and identities." Most events take place in Hampton Roads, Virginia.

www.ywow.org

866-876-YWOW (866-876-9969) or 757-468-2144

Comfort Zone Camp

Offers grief camps for children ages seven to twelve and thirteen to seventeen who have experienced the death of a loved one. Camps are usually in the Richmond, Virginia area. Camps are free and some travel scholarships are available.

www.ComfortZoneCamp.org

866-488-5679 or 804-377-3430

The Dougy Center for Grieving Children and Families

Provides peer support and information on grieving for children, teens, young adults and their families.

www.dougy.org

866-775-5683 or 503-775-5683

GriefNet
Online support group for anyone grieving a death or major loss.
www.griefnet.org

Military Widow: A survival guide
by Joanne M. Steen, MS, NCC and M. Regina Asaro, MS, RN, CT
Steen is the widow of a naval aviator who was killed in the line of duty.
The authors blend professional knowledge of grief and traumatic loss
with interviews with military widows, casualty officers, chaplains, and
command leaders.

Heart of a Hawk: One family's sacrifice & journey toward healing
by Deborah H. Tainsh
An honest and moving account of one family's journey through grief
following the death of their son in Iraq. Profits benefit TAPS.

The Hero in My Pocket
by Marlene Lee
A resource for children whose lives are affected by the death of a US
military service member.

*I'm Grieving As Fast As I Can: How young widows and widowers
can cope and heal*
by Linda Feinberg
Guides young widows and widowers through the grieving process while
highlighting the special circumstances of facing an untimely death.
Through stories, widows and widowers share their thoughts about
situations that arise as a result of losing a loved one, among them what
to tell young children, returning to work, and dealing with in-laws and
other relatives.

You Are Not Alone: Teens talk about life after the loss of a parent
by Lynne B Hughes
Lynne lost both parents at a young age. She is the founder of Comfort
Zone Camp. In this book, Lynne and her campers reach out to teens
and the people who care for them. Includes testimonials and comments
about what helps and what doesn't and ways to stay connected to a
loved one who has died.

The Five People You Meet in Heaven
by Mitch Albom
Eddie, an 83-year-old maintenance person at an amusement park, dies and meets five people in heaven. Each person's life and death was woven into Eddie's own in ways he never suspected. Through these five people, Eddie understands the meaning of his own life even as his arrival brings closure to theirs.

I Wasn't Ready to Say Goodbye: Surviving, coping and healing after the death of a loved one
by Brook Noel and Pamela D. Blair
The authors interview other tragedy survivors, share their own stories, and provide resources. Topics include the first few weeks, suicide, death of a child, when a body isn't found, children and grief, funerals and rituals, physical effects, homicide, and depression.

I Wasn't Ready to Say Goodbye Workbook: Surviving, coping and healing after the sudden death of a loved one (Workbook)
by Brook Noel and Pamela D. Blair
Workbook companion to the book.

Grief Steps: 10 steps to regroup, rebuild and renew after any life loss
by Brook Noel
Helps readers understand the steps they must take to rebuild, recover, and renew their lives when confronted by loss associated with death, divorce, relocation, and more.

Seven Choices: Finding daylight after loss shatters your world
by Elizabeth Harper Neeld
Maps the terrain between life as it was and life as it can be. Readers move at their own pace through the seven distinct phases of loss. Includes the author's own story of the loss of her young husband, the stories of other individuals, and research on coping with loss.

Healing a Spouse's Grieving Heart: 100 practical ideas after your husband or wife dies
by Alan D. Wolfelt, PhD
Activities and advice for widows and widowers. Easy-to-read format allows you think about and apply one idea at a time.

The Mourning Handbook: The most comprehensive resource...on all aspects of death and dying
by Helen Fitzgerald
Covers topics such as how long grief lasts, why it is important to express your grief, funeral preparations, mourning your loss, dealing with anniversaries and complicated grief issues, and being a friend to someone who is grieving.

A Time to Grieve: Meditations for healing after the death of a loved one
by Carol Staudacher
Daily thoughts and meditations about grief.

Grieving the Loss of Someone You Love: Daily meditations to help you through the grieving process
by Ray Mitsch and Lynn Brooksdie
A series of daily devotions. Helps readers understand the stages of grief; sort through the emotions of anger, guilt, fear and depression; and face the God who allowed their loss.

Angel Catcher
by Kathy Eldon and Amy Eldon
A guided journal to help a person who is grieving express their thoughts and remember the person who died.

Angel Catcher for Kids: A journal to help you remember the person who died
by Amy Eldon
A guided journal to help a child cope with the painful and often confusing process of grieving. Invites the child to record memories of the special person who died.

The Grieving Teen: A guide for teenagers and their friends
by Helen Fitzgerald
Helps teens understand the strong and difficult emotions they will experience and the new situations they will face after the death of a family member or friend, including family changes, issues with friends, problems at school, and the courage needed to move forward.

Fire in My Heart, Ice in My Veins: A journal for teenagers experiencing a loss
by Enid Samuel Traisman
A journal to help teens write letters, songs, and poems; tell the person who died what they want them to know; and use their creativity to work through the grieving process.

Healing Your Grieving Heart for Kids: 100 practical ideas
by Alan D. Wolfelt, PhD
Simple advice and activities to help children learn to express their grief and mourn naturally. Room to write or draw about feelings.

The Next Place
by Warren Hanson
A peaceful and hopeful picture book about what we might expect after leaving this life.

What's Heaven?
by Maria Shriver
A gentle children's story following the conversations that pass between a mother and a young daughter in the days immediately following the death of the child's special great-grandmother.

When Someone Very Special Dies: Children can learn to cope with grief
by Marie E. Heegaard
A guided journal for children to write and draw about their feelings. Helps young children understand the concepts of death, change, sadness, comfort, and coping through a life of change and growth.

Hotlines and Community Resources

Alcoholics Anonymous
Offers a self-help program for recovering alcoholics.
www.alcoholics-anonymous.org
212-870-3400

Al-Anon /Alateen
Offers support for family members and friends of alcoholics.
www.al-anon.alateen.org
888-425-2666

Child Abuse Hotline
24-hour hotline to help find local resources for children who are abused
or at risk of being abused.
www.childhelpusa.org
800-4-a-child (800-422-4453)

Narcotics Anonymous
Self-help organization for anyone recovering from drug addiction.
www.na.org
818-773-9999

National Domestic Violence Hotline
24-hour hotline for anyone facing domestic violence and anyone calling
on their behalf. Provide crisis intervention, safety planning, and referrals.
www.ndvh.org
800-799-SAFE (800-799-7233)

National Suicide Prevention Lifeline
24-hour hotline for anyone considering suicide and anyone calling on
their behalf.
www.suicidepreventionlifeline.org
800-273-TALK (800-273-8255)

Suicide Hotline / National Hopeline Network
24-hour hotline for anyone considering suicide and anyone calling on
their behalf. Web site has information about suicide and depression.
www.hopeline.com
800-SUICIDE (800-784-2433)

National Mental Health Association
Help for coping with tragic events, loss, and other topics.
www.nmha.org
703-684-7722
Resource center: 800-969-NMHA (800-969-6642)

Peer Military Groups and Veteran's Organizations

American Veterans (AMVETS)
Supports America's veterans and their communities through counseling and claims assistance, legislative action, and quality-of-life programs.
www.amvets.org
301-459-9600

American Legion
Provides assistance for veterans and survivors in filing and pursuing claims before the VA. Helps deployed service members' families with errands, household chores, or someone to talk to. Offers temporary financial assistance to help military families meet their children's needs.
www.legion.org
800-504-4098 or 202-861-2700

Disabled American Veterans
Services to America's veterans and service members include reviewing Medical Evaluation Board (MEB) results, representation before a Personnel Evaluation Board (PEB), and submission of claims before the VA for disability compensation, rehabilitation, and other benefits.
www.dav.org
877-I Am A Vet (877-426-2838) or 859-441-7300

Paralyzed Veterans of America
Works to maximize the quality of life for veterans and all people with spinal cord injury or disease.
www.pva.org
800-555-9140

Veterans of Foreign Wars
Legislative advocacy program that speaks out on Capitol Hill in support of service members, veterans and their families. Sponsors community service programs and special projects. Assists service members in procuring entitlements. Offers free phone cards to active-duty personnel.
www.vfw.org
816-756-3390

Veterans Service Organizations Directory
Lists organizations chartered by Congress or recognized by VA for claim representation.
www1.va.gov/vso